Breaking The Altar of Emotional Abuse

A Spiritual Guide to Emotional Freedom

Tara Jones-Roberson

even when I am exhausted. I could search the world and never find another man like you. Throughout this journey, you have seen me at my worst. You watched me hit rock bottom and rise back up. You witnessed my brokenness and my healing. You had a front-row seat to my battle with sobriety. Finally, you watched me transform into the woman I am today. I hope you are proud of me. I hope this book summarizes where we started and how much we have grown in Christ. I desire to inspire you as much as you inspire me. Because of you, I know what it means to love someone unconditionally. You never left me, and you never backed down, even when I threatened divorce for many years. My children could not have a more dedicated father. Words cannot express the rock you are for this family. I may not always say it, but I appreciate the order, cleanliness, and structure you bring to our home. Your hard work does not go unnoticed. I admire your unique attitude and how you separate yourself from worldly things. Although you don't always express it, I know you admire me too. I love you, babe! Our love is divine destiny!

Mother, I am grateful for your love, life lessons, and comical anecdotes. Your reputation for generosity and loyalty precedes you. You could have taught me many things, but you emphasized Jesus instead. It's the best thing you ever taught me. Your faith in Christ changed my life. I'm so grateful for all those Sunday mornings you required our attendance at church.

The unwillingness in me quickly transformed into passion and desire. I watched you shift through the storms of life, and although you made many mistakes, you never gave up. Now, I possess your strength and perseverance. We are very much alike, but also different. I am grateful that we can finally love and appreciate each other for who we are as individuals. Thank you for being a great mom. You deserve your heart's desires and much more.

To my dad: You have always been a light of inspiration to me. Growing up without your presence at home severely impacted me as a child. I am so glad that God restored our relationship. That is something many family relationships don't experience. I see so much of myself in you! My love for journalism, broadcast, music, travel, and country life comes from you. I will carry on the Jones name with pride and dignity. I will teach my children all about the bloodline, just like you taught me. You have always encouraged me to be different and think differently. Now is my time to show the world my difference. I love you, Daddy.

Growing up with my siblings was my life's best and worst times! I bet siblings all around the world feel the same way. Many of our memories are filled with love, joy, pain, and laughter. I hope our children will have as many inside jokes as we have. Sherrie, you were my second mom and my rock. You always had my back when it was up against a wall. Thank you for being a protector and inviting me along for the ride. As the years have passed, we have grown and changed from the girls we once were. Now we are adult women, raising families and pursuing different paths. One thing that has never changed is our love for one another. We don't always agree, but I'm thankful to know that I have a sister that will be there for me even when she disagrees with me! I pray that your many hidden talents will be revealed for the world to see! My constant desire is to be closer to you. I hope my book inspires you and confirms that you overcame emotional abuse. You have suffered much in your life, but you are an overcomer!

Kerry Jr., you are one of a kind! Your jokes and sense of humor will outlive you! The little brother I once had is now an adult man! Continue to grow and shine. Don't be afraid to shed the dead weight that often holds you down. You were made to soar!

You will be remembered as a legendary artist, but don't forget that God has given you more than just musical ability. Pursue your destiny and keep God first. You will be surprised to see everything he has in store for you! I hope my book inspires you to tell your own life story. There are many things that people don't know about you, and men all around the world need to hear them!

To my brother Marquez, you are truly missed! God worked through my grief to wake me up from the spiritual slumber I was in! For many years, I deceived myself into thinking I could hold on to my worldly ways and still claim Christ. Your death showed me that I needed to make a choice. I chose Christ, and now I'm all in! Your sacrifice gave me the momentum I needed to reach this season. I made it to my divine destiny because of you. I can still hear you saying, "Sis, God is going to bless us!" I'm at peace now because I know that God accepted you into the Kingdom of Heaven. You may have beat me there, but you can't get a crown until I get there! I dedicate this book of victory to you!

I hope the truth I tell and the revelations I give in this book will inspire my children to defy the odds and reach their God-given destinies no matter the cost. I dedicate this book to you all. You will not suffer in the same ways I have suffered, because I have gone before you in spirit and the world. The sacrifices that I have made for you benefit us all. You all changed my life and gave me a choice between mediocrity and greatness. I choose you all every time, and you all are great! Carry my torch well. Let's make history together as the Roberson family!

I also want to dedicate this book to every prophet, pastor, leader, apostle, or teacher that has poured into me! Ministry saved my life! Thank you to my spiritual parents, Apostle Omar Morton and Prophetess Makita Morton. Your ministry helped me to break through! Thanks to coach Sophia Ruffin and the Ready Writer platform that she created! Your obedience and vision birthed my childhood desire and divine purpose of being a writer!

Lastly, this book is dedicated to every woman who has been tried in the fire and has a promise from God to come out gold. I am proof that you can do everything through Christ who strengthens you! Don't quit, don't give up, don't give in! The devil will regret going to war with you! There is much joy after this!

"Be brave, be strong and courageous. Do not be afraid. Do not be discouraged. For the Lord, your God will be with you wherever you go." Joshua 1:1

CONTENTS

Dedication i

Preface ix

Prayer xiii

Chapter 1: The Foundation of Emotional Abuse 1

Chapter 2: Reinforcement & Revealing of Spirits 15

Chapter 3: Identity Theft 42

Chapter 4: Healing From the Pain, Restoring What Was Lost ... 52

Chapter 5: Transforming Pity Into Purpose 60

Chapter 6: Overcoming Victim Mentality, Walking in Victory .. 69

Chapter 7: Woman of God Walking in Her Divine Destiny 78

PREFACE

This book exists because of the silent warfare and emotional trauma that women experience throughout their lifetimes. Women worldwide suffer emotional abuse in marriage, childhood, family relationships, friendships, and even in the job force. Sadly, I have experienced all of these. My experiences led to the birth of this book. Now, I am a mirror for other women who need hope and understanding. Looking in the rearview mirror, I can see how every burden worked for my good.

Contrarily, it didn't always feel like it was working for my good. Many times, I thought I would lose my mind. There were many days when I wanted to curl up and die. The pain I have experienced from being disconnected from my spouse, mother, siblings, church members, and even friends created a deep level of despair and desperation in me. Now, I can relate to other women who carry the same burden.

The primary purpose of this book is to give hope and inspiration and to motivate women to "Get Up and Live!" I hope to guide women to their predestined purpose. I want women worldwide to know that they have power in Christ. We are not subject to worldly fate, emotional triggers, or childhood trauma. I want men to read my book and understand the power of their words over their wives and families. My greatest desire is to see men come to Christ and lead their families to victory! If children should read my book, I hope it will teach them to walk in total confidence. They should know that no matter what people say about them, it is okay to be themselves, love God, and pursue their dreams. God loves us all very much, and because he is so confident in his abilities to renew and restore us, he will allow us to go through the fire to save someone else.

After being in that fire for so long, I finally had the wisdom, confidence, and opportunity I needed to complete heavenly assignments. Prophetess Sophia Ruffin gave the clarion call to join Ready Writer, and I gladly accepted. I put my bank account into overdraft, and spent every dollar I had left to partake in the six-week writer's challenge. For once, I bet on myself. I put myself first and supported this invisible dream that no one else could see. I pushed through so many challenges to complete this book! The warfare against me increased while my finances decreased. The spirit of torment was released over my children and me during this writing process.

I also encountered thoughts of suicide, increased levels of sleep deprivation, financial ruin, mental warfare, mental stress, severe body aches, and self-doubt. Above all else, I encountered God! I experienced the glory of his strength and faithfulness. This book came to pass because the Lord spoke through me despite my physical circumstances. He challenged me to a six-week accelerated writing course that ushered me into a new season. God plans to heal, reveal, and encourage others.

Men and women should read this book because it is a guide to spiritual and emotional freedom. Married couples will be inspired to stay together and grow in God. Married women will see that carrying the burden of their families is not a vain act. Married men will be motivated to grow closer to God and accept their high calling in Jesus Christ. Men will have a clear view of the power in their mouths. Single people will see what relationships look like after the honeymoon phase. They will also learn why making Christ the foundation of marriage is so important.

Anyone who has experienced abusive words or lacks confidence in themselves can relate to this book. They will connect if they don't have healthy boundaries set in their lives or if they have let others take advantage of them. I think everyone has experienced emotional abuse at some point, but the severity level varies by person. My book will reveal the demonic spirits responsible for domestic violence. After reading, you should no longer be stuck in the natural mind frame of solely blaming the physical abuser instead of acknowledging the actual abuser: Satan. Upon reading this book, prepare to be healed, delivered, and set free from emotional abuse! That's what *Breaking the Altar of Emotional Abuse* has done for me!

PRAYER

Thank you, Jesus, for every person that reads this book. I pray that this book will be strategically placed into the hands of every person who needs my information. Every man, woman, boy, and girl that reads this book will be blessed. Holy Spirit, I pray that you will enter their hearts and cause them to experience your love and goodness. May they encounter the peace, revelation, and wisdom of God. I pray that this book will stop them in their tracks and place them on the path of righteousness and integrity. I pray for the spirit of a winner to be released over them. May the heart of a finisher be released over them. I pray that endurance, perseverance, and the character of Christ will come upon them because of this book.

I declare that marriages will be restored. Self-image will be restored, and mental illness will be dismantled. False identity will be shattered in the name of Jesus Christ. May this book renew relationships, open the door to divine purpose, and create new levels of faith. After all that, Lord, please don't stop there. Please put it in their hearts and spirits to share this book so that people worldwide, especially women, can be set free from the snare of emotional abuse. May every demonic alliance against my readers be defeated in the name of Jesus. Open their eyes as they read and pierce their hearts to receive the truth and the love of Jesus Christ. I pray that success, faith, goodness, healing, restoration, rededication, and forgiveness will be the result of this book. Let the anointing from your spirit flow freely through the pages. Thank you, Father, for choosing me and for keeping me. It has been an honor to go through this process with you. I pray that they feel the sincerity coming from my heart. Amen.

Chapter 1

THE FOUNDATION OF EMOTIONAL ABUSE

I have experienced emotional abuse since I was a child. In the past, there wasn't a name to classify emotional or verbal abuse. People called it a "mood," or would say, "You know how he/she is." In this century and generation, it has been widely experienced and is now defined. Emotional, verbal, and physical abuse are all forms of domestic violence. A demonic power sustains domestic violence. The branch of emotional abuse has a spiritual undertone that is always hidden and hushed. Because the spiritual aspect goes untaught, the cycle of domestic violence rages on. Defining *abuse* is critical, but so is the need to move past a single definition.

Abuse is the cruel or violent treatment of a person or animal. It is also defined as using something to harmful effect or for a bad purpose. In this case, it is improperly using a person's emotions. Synonyms for abuse include: to take advantage of, mistreat, misuse, mishandle, or pervert. In Jeremiah 29:11, the Bible says God has a good purpose for us. The definition of abuse refers to using something for a bad purpose, so immediately, we can see that abuse is a demonic strategy that the devil uses to destroy God's purpose for his children. We know Satan plans to steal, kill, and destroy us. Therefore, he has an evil purpose for us. Thus, emotional abuse is a tool that Satan uses to destroy self-love, self-confidence, divine purpose, mental stability, and unity in marriage and other relationships. It's critical to highlight the definition of abuse so that it can directly relate to emotional health.

Another term worthy of defining is the term *altar*. An altar is a table used as the focus of a religious ritual, especially for making sacrifices or offerings to a deity. A spiritual altar is either utilized for Christ or the devil. Emotional abuse is a spiritual altar that can be raised by oneself or the enemy. Several different sacrifices or offerings cause the altar to be uplifted within our life. Accepting Satan's lies, Engaging in sin, unbroken generational curses, and unhealed trauma are a few reasons why the altar can be raised. The two terms together create the altar of emotional abuse. When this altar is raised in your life, you will experience constant turmoil. This altar causes you to be unstable in your mind, your feelings, and your heart. Your thoughts become consumed with the abuser(s) and why they say certain things. Your days become consumed with your abuser's behavior. Often you "walk on eggshells," waiting for and expecting the next explosion or attack.

You may even feel the spirit of fear looming around you and your home. It can feel as though you don't know what to do or say. You may feel afraid of what the abuser will say or how they will act if you do or say certain things. The day, the week, the month, and even your life hinge upon the abuser's mood. Depression will even try to creep in.

Emotional abuse is a sad and grim reality. However, it is necessary to acknowledge and identify it. Then, you can defeat it and attain spiritual freedom. When I refer to emotional abuse, I am including verbal abuse. Verbal and emotional abuse are two different things, but they work together. Emotional abuse begins with negative words that stem from verbal abuse. Anger provokes words. Words provoke emotions. Emotions provoke actions. This formula is the foundation of emotional abuse.

Here is the backstory of my foundation in verbal abuse and how it transformed into emotional abuse. Yours may or may not be similar, but the same foundational principles apply. As you are reading about my childhood experiences, consider your own experiences. Consider your foundation with verbal or emotional abuse. Where did it start?

Many women and men have s similar story of being raised in a broken home. Like many others, I am a product of divorce, which left me in a single-parent home. My mother eventually remarried, and I had two parents in the household. That marriage ultimately dissolved too, bringing me back to a single-parent home. One thing that remained the same, despite the physical dynamics of our home, was my mother's explosive attitude.

I want to highlight something important here. Although my mother was the initial person to introduce me to "abusive language," you must understand the spiritual side of things. Within every physical situation, there is a spirit at work. If you are not in a close relationship with the Holy Spirit, you will not know the evil spirits fighting you. Without this insight, you will consider your situation purely physical. You solely blame the "abuser" or the person causing the harm. Although that person is responsible for their words, actions, and reactions, they may also be under the influence of a demonic spirit. Quite often, we are influenced by demonic spirits unknowingly. Think about times when you have said or done things that you regret. When you think back, you may realize how deeply it affected someone. Maybe it has affected someone more than you even know. The enemy has a way of using people's words or actions to bring discouragement to believers and unbelievers. Satan does not want the believer to grow, nor does he want the non-believer to receive the life-changing gift of salvation.

So, any person can be influenced by the spirit of God or by demonic spirits. Spirits are always influencing us; the question is, which ones?

Ephesians 6:12 says, *"Our struggle is not against flesh and blood* [contending only with physical opponents], *but against the rulers, against the powers, against the world forces of this* [present] *darkness, against the spiritual forces of wickedness in the heavenly* (supernatural) *places."*

This verse indicates a sinister force we cannot see is working against us. People are not our enemies. Our enemies are the evil spirits influencing people. Therefore, we cannot solely focus on material things. We must dig deeper into the spiritual. This may be why you cannot move past your situation. You have yet to realize that the spiritual realm is more powerful than our physical realm.

There is an enemy of your soul lurking and waiting for the perfect opportunity to discourage you, destroy you, and abolish your purpose. As you are reading, focus on the spirit at work, not the person influenced by the spirit. Use this technique in your personal life as well. Acknowledging the spiritual aspect will shift your thinking and make room for forgiveness. Most people struggle to accept this perspective, but if you want freedom, you need to receive it as the hidden truth that will set you free.

In many ways, my mother was similar to other mothers. She had the same goals as most. She wanted to provide for her children, raise us in a safe environment, and ensure we received a decent education. Although my mother was a Christian woman dedicated to the church, she had her struggles, problems, and trials. Raising five kids alone was not an easy feat. She was often overworked, lacked sleep, and had to maintain life with the world's stress on her shoulders. Even though my mother's children were the best part of her life, we also seemed to be an emotional trigger. As we grew older, every little thing seemed to set her off. Of course, children have a way of pushing their parents' tempers to the limit, but it appeared that even the small things would cause her to explode with word curses.

I longed for my mother's love, but it always felt so far away. The more I wanted to be close to her, the more her words seemed to cut like a knife. Immediately, in the spirit, I was being rejected, but in the natural,

I was connecting with emotional and verbal abuse. Rejection became the key to the door of suppression.

My childhood foundation was imparting rejection and suppression in me. Impartation is the point of receiving something intangible as tangible. Impartation causes your belief system to be activated, shifting your thinking patterns to believe in the things you consider to be truth or lies. Impartation shapes your perspective. As a child, I was shaped and molded by the negative words I constantly heard. The emotional standard in my family was suppression. We did not discuss traumatic events or hurtful occurrences. As a family, we did not communicate our feelings or lack thereof. There weren't many opportunities to express anger or other emotions healthily. There were no guidelines to teach us how to cope emotionally. This is the point where verbal abuse became emotional abuse. I was attacked verbally and oppressed emotionally.

Because of this emotionally hostile environment, I learned to suppress what I felt or shut down emotionally. My siblings and I were usually ridiculed and rejected when we tried to talk to our mom about how we felt. It was quickly swept under the rug and ignored. The silent treatment became my most excellent tool, so I would internalize how I felt and not talk about it. This was very unhealthy for me. Suppression molded me into a quiet storm. I would hold it in when things hurt or bothered me and let it build up. Finally, I would explode in anger when I couldn't take anymore. It's hard to calm down once you are pushed to that level. This level is the climax of the unhealthy effects of suppression. It is usually birthed out of fear. Because I suppressed my emotions, I could never effectively communicate what I was feeling. I feared getting in trouble or being ignored. In some areas, this even caused me to be timid. Now, I can see how suppression affected my level of communication with men, my desire to be loved, and even my timidity with public speaking. If you're struggling with suppression or have struggled with any of this in the past, then repeat this prayer:

"Father in Heaven, protect my mind, emotions, and spirit from the lies of the enemy. I break the stronghold of emotional suppression. I am free this day! Thank you for revealing my triggers from the past. I acknowledge them and release myself from them. My emotions are stable in Jesus' name. I cancel the spirit of rejection and fear! I have authority and freedom in Christ. I can open my mouth and speak the truth of God. I speak boldly! I say what I feel in the moment and do not bottle up my emotions. I dismantle the yoke of suppression by the blood of Jesus Christ! Amen."

When I was a young girl, fear, suppression, and rejection were detrimental to my emotional stability. Collectively, these things led to emotional triggers. As a child, I was triggered to sadness and suppression when I heard these words and sayings:

"Fat girl"
"Speak only when spoken to."
"Because I said so."
"Crybaby"
"What happens in this house stays in this house."

> "You're too sensitive."
> "Be seen and not heard."
> "Do as I say and not as I do."
> "You have a terrible attitude and a bad disposition about yourself."
> "Just a mean-spirited girl"

These words rang in my ears more times than I could count. They are all tactics from Satan. Another tactic that Satan works through is sarcasm. This can be hidden abuse within the family. It's easy to overlook it because of its comical appeal. But it's critical to identify it properly. When sarcasm becomes coarse (mean, malicious, demeaning), it is a form of verbal abuse. I don't know if we understood this as kids, because sarcasm and "joking" were widely used in my home. Like many, we were a family of pranksters and jokesters. I like to think that we laughed the pain away.

In some cases, this coping mechanism is okay. The Bible says that laughter is good for the heart. In the Bible, it is compared to medicine. Therefore, there is nothing wrong with joking and having fun. Kevin Hart even named his comedy special "Laugh at My Pain." However, "coarse joking" is inappropriate, and it is dangerous.

My siblings and I perfected the art of using sarcasm and jokes as ammunition. We would sometimes harm each other with our words to the point of tears. And I'm not referring to tears of joy. As I grew older, I realized how unhealthy it was. The effects of verbal abuse encouraged us to use our jokes to tear each other down. Why is it that a joke is only funny if it degrades someone?

This is dangerous because you will begin to use sarcasm as a cover-up for what you really feel and want to say. Because of fear, it is easier to express feelings through a joke. Because of rejection, it is easier to communicate by using sarcasm as a shield to protect one from being ignored. We did not know how to define what we were experiencing emotionally, so we would sarcastically say things like, "Crazy Joe is on the warpath again." We were referring to the movie *Lean on Me*. In my home, my mother was like the principal, Joe Clark, in the movie. Television and film are big on sarcasm, and it helped us describe what we were experiencing. My mother would refer to us as "The Addams Family" to describe the dysfunction in our home. Sarcasm can be abusive, confusing, and damaging. This type of family abuse is common and is usually hidden. It is a mask that covers broken communication skills and low self-esteem.

Mother played a double role in my emotional formation. Her verbal attacks and low self-esteem were the foundation of my brokenness. This caused the very breach in my spirit that Satan needed to gain access to my emotions. I was affected emotionally by my mother's struggle with her skin condition. When I was a freshman in high school, my mother was diagnosed with lupus. Her skin was deeply affected. She began to have outbreaks that completely changed her facial appearance Her skin tone became darker, and her clear, smooth skin became bumpy and swollen. I saw a massive change in her confidence level.

Although it is understandable that she would lose confidence in her image, I expected her to be assured. I was just a young girl and had no idea of the depth of what she was facing. I only knew what I felt. I didn't realize I had set such high expectations for her.

My mother possessed the strength of an ox. She kept going to work and providing for us while facing daily disappointment and embarrassment. Seeing her in this vulnerable state, I began to understand why my mother was so explosive in her nature. Suddenly, I could see the pain she always carried. I could see the brokenness that was present before her skin was compromised. My mother was never a quiet woman, so she always verbalized how she felt. Her children were her audience, and we watched and listened to the shattering of her self-confidence.

I internalized all of this. She said things like:

> "I'm so ugly now."
> "I look like the Loch Ness Monster."
> "I used to be beautiful like you."
> "I wish I was pretty like you."
> "My skin used to look like yours."

She would completely demean herself with her own words and compliment me and my sister in the same breath.

> "I have some beautiful girls."
> "Your skin is so soft and pretty."
> "You should be a model."

Internally, I struggled with the verbiage. Inside I thought to myself,

I look just like my mom, so am I pretty or ugly? My mom became obsessed with her skin and how she could fix it. She withdrew from the church and felt ashamed when none of the members reached out to her. I sympathized with her, and I felt the same pain she felt. Naturally, I began to struggle with my self-esteem and identity. I started questioning who I was, whom I wanted to be, and why I felt the way I felt. Because of fear, I could not confide in my mother about these things. This enacted the "Sensitivity Search."

My family always called me sensitive because I was quick to cry or get emotional. During high school, I wanted answers to my questions about myself. I always felt things very deeply. Everything was so mystical. I always possessed "deep emotion" and needed to understand why I felt what I felt. Regardless of what the emotion was, it was intensified. It could have just been puberty or feminine hormones. Whatever it was, I wanted answers.

The internet was still young, and so was my mind. I explored different internet searches about "deep thinkers," "overemotional," and "sensitive feelings." Eventually, I ran into astrology and horoscopes. I began to identify with the "sensitivity" of Pisces.

It perfectly described my feelings and personality, so I agreed with it. I followed my horoscope religiously! I signed up for emails. I would even check it online every day.

You may be wondering what this has to do with emotional abuse? Well, astrology set the stage for me to accept the instability of my feelings and emotions. Because I agreed with whatever the horoscope suggested, my emotional make-up hinged upon the reading for the day. If my horoscope said it would be an emotional day, I would expect it to be an emotional day. If the reading said, "Today is a good day for happiness, and you will be surprised by your new excitement," I agreed. Essentially, my spirit opened to the reality that everything controlled my emotions but me. Horoscopes and astrology taught me that those external things controlled my feelings—not me, not God.

The truth is that it's okay to experience and process emotions, but it's not okay to be controlled by them. An outside source shouldn't dictate how you feel every day. I was accepting a false prophecy. I allowed astrology to determine my days and my future. That is God's place. Jesus is the original prophet. Prophecy and insight into the future come from him, no other source. This was a great set-up from the evil one. My belief system was infiltrated, and my identity was officially breached. Immature thinking and identity crisis allowed the altar of emotional abuse to be raised in my life. With this demonic altar raised in my life, I was the perfect recipient of continued abuse and the damaging effects it brings. Satan's diabolical plan was to destroy me emotionally and connect me with a false identity that did not leave room for Christ.

You cannot control what other people do or say. And when you do control others, you are operating in witchcraft. However, you can control whether you identify with, agree with, and accept what others do and say. The instability of emotions had taken root in me.

Emotional abuse becomes familiar with the instability that it brings. The abuser is upset today, but tomorrow they are okay. The next day they are sad. So on and so on. You are exposed to all of this, and it becomes "familiar." This is called the workings of "familiar spirits." When you normalize your feelings' constant up-and-down movement, your feelings are never stable. Now any little thing can cause you to be sad or moody. The workings of "familiar spirits" are deeply involved in emotional abuse. You don't just wake up and become abused. At some point, you accept it because of previous pain, trauma, or familiarity.

You must consider your foundation in emotional abuse—question yourself for a few moments. Reflect on your past. What happened to you as a child? When did the breach in your identity occur? Is there a current breach in your identity? Are you following other sources and beliefs outside of Christ? If so, what are they? Why do you follow them, and how did you get exposed to them? Who are the role players in your foundation? How did you get to the point of emotional abuse? What is your level of self-esteem? What controls your emotions? Is it TV, music, or entertainment?

These are just a few questions, but I encourage you to dig deeper. If necessary, journal your experience. Take more time to contemplate the foundation of the emotional and verbal abuse you have suffered. Now, consider the importance of the emotional foundation in your life. In general, why is a solid foundation necessary? The purpose of a solid foundation is to build something. If the foundation is not strong, the building will collapse. An intense storm will come along, and everything will come tumbling down. This happens to us when our foundation is not built on Christ.

The storms and trials of life will blow on us until we crumble and break down. In this case, the storm and trials are emotional and verbal abuse. The objects that crumble and break down are our self-confidence, self-esteem, self-love, and even our drive and passion for life. If we are not careful to guard and rebuild our foundation on Christ, we risk living unfulfilled lives. We run the risk of living a cynical and pessimistic life. We indeed have the human power to put the pieces back together ourselves. However, some parts will still be broken, and others will be misplaced. With Christ, we can be whole, happy, and completely restored. You can't choose your childhood foundation, but you have the power to decide how you rebuild your new foundation.

Remember this:
Satan always attacks anointed children and their parents. He uses them against each other. If you had an abnormal upbringing, it was on purpose. Satan purposed it to ruin you, but God will use it to develop your spiritual character. The devil hates anointed, gifted, and chosen people. He especially hates their families because two are stronger than one. Unity is better than independence. I was an anointed child, but family members, friends, and church members did not identify it. They only knew I was different. I love my mother and family very much. They did not realize that they needed to stand in prayer for me, but now that I understand it, I intercede for them.

Chapter 2

REINFORCEMENT & REVEALING OF SPIRITS

I met my husband in 2013. My son Malik was ten months old. I had transferred home to Memphis from Middle Tennessee State University the prior year. I was just getting established in my family housing on campus. My husband was a family friend, but somehow, I'd never met him before. We fell in love quickly; it was love at first sight. Malik connected with my husband immediately. My relationship with Malik's father was over, and I was ready to build a family. My husband felt the same way about us. Our relationship progressed quickly. Within six months, we were living together.

At the time, his house caught on fire, and he needed temporary shelter. I was excited to help my newfound love, so he moved in with Malik and me. We quickly meshed as a family, and we all loved it. After a few months, his home was restored and rebuilt. But in a short time, I grew to love him more, and I knew he loved me the same way. Things were going so well that I did not want him to move out. I asked him to stay. I prayed many times and knew that God revealed that he was my husband. He also knew that I was his wife. We agreed to wait until I graduated to get married. I graduated from college in May of 2015. We got married in August 2016.

Before we were married, I saw his flaws, and he saw mine. We quickly learned each other's strengths, weaknesses, and habits. By now, the honeymoon phase was over, and we were settling into everyday life with each other. Our first fight was about something small and petty. That was the first time I saw his personality change, and that was the first time he saw my unstable reactions.

Nevertheless, we both passed it off as no big deal. We should not have ignored the red flags. Although we knew we were meant to be together, we should have addressed the emotionally unhealthy tone we were setting for our marriage.

Arguments should not lead to disrespectful, unloving, and unkind words. They shouldn't lead to dangerous physical reactions either. This shows the power of words and triggers. From the beginning, we accepted the invitation into a demonic cycle. We approved the methods of our arguing. Instead, we should have set boundaries. We should have discussed the root causes driving our reactions and provoking words. We didn't do any of those things. We forgave and moved on. That is not the appropriate way to deal with unhealthy words and behaviors. This cycle continued for several years.

Because we did not have a solid prayer life, we were susceptible to unidentified spiritual warfare. We are both Christian believers, but I had the most experience. I had previous encounters with God, and I could still hear the voice of the Holy Spirit. However, I was in denial about the sin in my life, and I had become very carnal (worldly/fleshly). I was mixing the world's ways with God's spiritual principles. I was mixing sin with holiness. I included my bad habits and "stinking thinking" into my prayer life and intimate time with God. My addictions got worse after my brother died.

Suddenly, I needed to smoke as soon as I woke up. I could barely get my kids out the door for school without taking a puff of a Black and Mild cigar. That was followed by marijuana use throughout the entire day. Before praying, I would bring my ashtray to my prayer closet and smoke Black and Mild cigars. My habit was that bad. However, I still enjoyed the presence of God and prayer. I didn't want to give up my relationship with God, but I didn't want to give up my bad habits either. This is how the two began to mix. I was experiencing the true meaning of the phrase "Come to God as you are."

Finally, one day I was in my prayer space, putting my cigar out before prayer. The Lord spoke to me so softly. "Why don't you just own it?" I smiled. Somewhere in my twisted mind, I thought God was finally approving my smoking habit. I deceived myself into believing that smoking was not that bad and that I needed it. In prayer, I gave God all these reasons why I couldn't quit, why I didn't want to quit, and how smoking helped my anxiety. God was always so patient in listening. He had never spoken about it until now. He gave me clarity and said, "You need to own the fact that you can't quit without me."

At that moment, I became conscious of the sin in my life. God was calling me to holiness. My thinking began to shift, and the process of sobriety would start soon. What areas in your life need to be completely yielded to God?

My marriage had become bittersweet. We still had so much love and passion, but we could not get along. We would fight about minor things. Even when the issues were significant, the results were always the same. My husband would yell and curse. He was unkind and unloving with his words. I would slam doors and throw or break things. Malik and our daughter Makyla witnessed these things. This behavior was increasingly unhealthy for the whole family. After a big blow-up, we would numb the pain with marijuana and block it out with the silent treatment. Of course, I was the best at the silent treatment. This habit was so natural from childhood, so it was always easy to ignore him for a week. Especially since I was still bitter about what he had previously said. Sporadically, I would try to talk to him about the issues, but he was more bitter than I. He would say things like, "It doesn't matter; I'm so used to it," and "It's never going to change; it is what it is." Those conversations would leave me feeling hopeless. They made me feel like everything was my fault, and there was no way out of this cycle.

My husband's bitterness showed up as cold-heartedness. He seemed to be emotionally void. I knew this had much to do with his past, not just what he experienced with me. Some days he would wake up angry, with a different demeanor and personality. It was more profound than just anger. Some days it was all doom and gloom. It's like a switch would go off. He would transition from comical, fun-loving Pat to cynical, condescending Pat. His words were provoking and belittling. Sometimes it felt like he wanted me to feel the pain. In my mind, he knew these things hurt me, but he kept saying them repeatedly to ensure I heard him. Although I was conscious of the sin in my life, I still hadn't dealt with it. I was still unwilling to give up my ways and my habits. Because of this, I could not see the red flags of spiritual warfare. The enemy had used my mother against me as a child. Now he was using my husband against me.

The battles in my marriage reinforced my subconscious reasoning for suppression. My husband reinforced all the verbal trauma I suffered as a child. His words pushed the knife deeper into my heart. In the past, my mother's words triggered sadness and suppression, but my husband's words triggered me to anger. The aggressive verbiage bought me a ticket on an emotional roller coaster that I did not want to ride.

My mother and spouse both had similar emotional qualities. They were controlling, overbearing, explosive, and closed-off. As an adult woman, I was triggered to fear, anger, bitterness, and sadness when I heard these words from my spouse:

"Hypocrite"
"Fake Christian"
"Bad Mom"
"You're just like everybody else."
"This is a terrible family."

> "I feel like a dead man."

My heart shattered over and over every time I heard these words. He would raise his defense mechanism whenever I tried to bring attention to his abusive words. Since he was a young boy, his tongue and words had been his defense. He would point out all my flaws, even things that had nothing to do with the current issue. His defense mechanism protected him from accepting responsibility for his words. Just like in my childhood, I was rejected and afraid to speak.

One night I was so angry with him that I decided to sleep on the couch. Previously, if I ever fell asleep on the couch, he would come and wake me and bring me to bed like a baby. I enjoyed it. I even thought it was sweet. So, I was shocked when he exploded because I slept on the couch out of frustration. That thing with his personality change was happening again. He paced back and forth around the couch. It was intimidating.

> "Is that what God told you to do? God doesn't make you sleep away from your husband."
>
> "That's how I know it's fake. I'll never serve that kind of God."

My relationship with God always became the focus. I was constantly mocked and humiliated for being a Christian and trying to get closer to God. He continued for a while until I finally got in the bed just to make it stop. I cried myself to sleep that night, full of fear and dread. After that, I knew something disturbing was working within my husband. Indeed, I was about to identify it.

Things had gotten so bad that I was ready to divorce. I would always tell him that I wanted a divorce, and now I was prepared to do it. God would always say, "No, stay."

I couldn't believe God was witnessing the abuse I was suffering, and he was okay with it. This is when mental warfare kicked into high gear. I would say to myself, "Maybe I am crazy." "This isn't God. God doesn't let you suffer like this." "It's not God's plan for me to be abused." One day, I was online researching divorce, and the Lord led me on another search. It came to my mind to research "men's emotion." I googled things like, "Why is my spouse so mean?" Finally, I came across an article about narcissistic personality disorder. When I read the signs and symptoms, I was appalled! It was everything I had experienced up to that point! It was so much confirmation. Yet, it made me so sad. I was broken-hearted all over again. I had so many questions. "Why was I experiencing this?" "Why is God telling me to stay?" "Is this God?" At that moment, I truly realized how much pain, trauma, and abuse I had suffered. I only wanted a divorce to make the painful cycles stop. I didn't consider how it would affect my children or that God was doing a great work within me. Up to that point, I had not acknowledged my situation. Now, I was identifying it. Little did I know that God was not telling me my husband had NPD. He was revealing the narcissist spirit to me. It was only one of many demonic spirits that were in alliance against me.

I still did not know that I was being emotionally manipulated. I prepared for the verbal attacks in between debating with God about divorce. I tried to do everything his way so that he wouldn't explode. I was living in fear, but I wasn't afraid for my life. I was afraid of what he would say. Self-doubt consumed me. "Should I do this? Will this make him mad? I shouldn't say this, or he will get mad, then I will get mad, and once I get mad, everything will get worse." Mental anguish was my new norm.

I dreaded holidays and special occasions. They were the worst. Every holiday, we would fight. I expressed how much I loved gifts and birthdays, yet he never celebrated them with me. Most of the time, he wouldn't say "Happy Birthday." I always prepared myself mentally before the special day would come. I expected a fight or silent treatment or an attitude change. My emotions were being manipulated because I was presented with the option to stop loving myself. The notion of self-worth loomed around me constantly.

Now my thoughts were:

> "You're not even worth a Valentine's Day gift."
> "You must not be a good mom if he won't say Happy Mother's Day."
> "He doesn't love you."

For a long time, I blamed my husband for everything. "If he didn't provoke me, I wouldn't respond with anger. If he didn't treat me so bad, I wouldn't feel this way." It seemed that he was the source of all my pain. For many years, bitterness consumed me. I could not fathom that the one responsible for loving me was the same one who was causing me undeniable pain. I had given this man my home, children, body, money, time, and so much more. "How could he do me like this? Why is he doing me like this? Don't I deserve better than this?"

I was in so much pain that I didn't take the time to figure out why my husband was so disconnected. Whenever I would ponder on it, I understood some of it. I knew a lot about his past and what he had experienced. Nevertheless, I was so entangled in my pain that I could not always sympathize with him. But if I had gotten off the pity train, I would have realized that the verbal abuse was an indicator of my husband's own pain and issues. His identity had been breached, too. In a sense, the abuse isn't about you. It's about the abuser's trauma, pain, and insecurities. This made him an available host for demonic spirits to work through. These spirits wanted to devour me, and he gave them direct access. Often, my reactions to his words would trigger him to his past and leave him feeling hopeless about life. This is the assignment of demonic spirits. They keep your mind stuck in the past while diligently destroying your future.

As I mentioned before, I was constantly debating with God about divorce. At some point, God revealed to me that my husband was my heavenly assignment and he allowed me to suffer with a plan and purpose in mind. Is your abuser your assignment? Believe it or not, some hellish relationships are sent from Heaven. Identify the relationships in your life. It's pointless to be abused without a purpose. The only way you will know your relationships are from God is if he confirms them.

Relationships aren't always transparent. It can look like roses and peaches, but it can hinder your life. It can be full of hell and make you run for the hills, but it's the very thing you need to attain growth and maturity. That's why it's imperative to develop a relationship with God. He can reveal answers to you in many different forms.

He can speak through dreams, people, music, tv, books, and even babies. For a period, God communicated with me through letters that I wrote to a church in another state. Anything is possible with God. He is not limited to one pastor in a church. But you can't receive if you aren't in tune, and you aren't listening. Whether you know your assignment or purpose or are blind to it, Hell's Kingdom is out to destroy it.

I will continue to reveal the demonic nature of emotional abuse. It is a satanic strategy and stronghold sent to block your destiny (God's purpose for your life).

> *"'For I know the plans and thoughts that I have for you,' says the Lord, 'plans for peace and well-being and not for disaster, to give you a future and a hope.'"* Jeremiah 29:11

> *"Just as* [in His love] *He chose us in Christ* [actually selected us for Himself as His own] *before the foundation of the world, so that we would be holy* [that is, consecrated, set apart for Him, purpose-driven] *and blameless in His sight."* Ephesians 1:4

Before the foundations of the world were established, God created you with a divine purpose in mind. Satan's three-fold ministry is to kill, steal, and destroy your purpose before it is birthed, activated, and fulfilled. He will do this by any means necessary. Therefore, emotional abuse is like a spiritual bully. But not like the one on the playground. That bully has something to prove. This one doesn't. Satan isn't trying to prove anything; he is trying to accomplish his goals.

KINGDOM OF DARKNESS AGENDA

1. **Pull you out of the Spirit**- It's impossible to be in the spirit (in prayer, meditation, love, peaceful demeanor) and be angry simultaneously. The Bible says to be slow to anger.

   "For the [resentful, deep-seated] *anger of man does not produce the righteousness of God* [that standard of behavior which He requires from us]." James 1:20

   God understands that anger ruins and influences our character in the worst way. So many times, I let the enemy pull me out of the spirit. In certain instances, I went willingly. Other times I was provoked. I had to mature in spiritual things before I realized that God is willing and able to fight my battles. But he won't fight them if you're already in the ring. Ultimately, I was fighting a spirit, not my husband. And evil spirits understand that if you are fighting them in the physical realm, you won't have time to dwell with God in the spiritual realm. And you won't have time to grow with God. The enemy's plan is to keep you consumed with what he/she did to hurt you in hopes of stunting your growth.

2. **Cause deep-rooted depression and sadness**- The devil loves depression. It almost embodies him. It's full of darkness, doom, gloom, suicide, and mental warfare, which is related to mental

illness. The Bible has so many scriptures about joy, peace, and love. This is the fruit of the spirit. God always wants to see us joyful. He desires us to be happy, healthy, and whole. The devil desires the opposite for us because he is the opposer. Many times, I gave up on my situation and wallowed in misery, believing that there was no way out. This is a classic sign of depression. Have you ever seen a deeply sad person rise to their greatest potential? Do people who suffer from depression have the motivation needed to achieve divine purpose? Do they have zeal and passion for life? The demonic kingdom knows these things and capitalizes on them.

3. **Satan wants to mute you**- Everything in life and the kingdom of God is voice-activated! One of the effects of verbal and emotional abuse is fear. It's easy to become paralyzed with fear and lose confidence in your words. For a period of time, I stopped talking to my spouse completely. Unless it was about the kids or bills, we didn't talk. I was afraid of what he would say. I was afraid of what I would do if he said the wrong thing. I started to think no one cared about what I thought or what I had to say. Satan is a master manipulator and liar. He wants to muzzle you so that you don't find your power. There is power in your voice! There is power in the word of God! The word must be spoken to be activated! Speak the word with authority!

4. **Satan wants you to run in fear**- The Bible says "Fear Not" three hundred and sixty-five times. God is confident in his ability, and he wants you to be confident in him as well. It is okay to separate

yourself from certain situations or people, but it's not okay to run away. These are two different things. Separation is a sign of consecration, and consecration is separation for God's purposes. Running away from uncomfortable situations is a result of anger, frustration, or bitterness. God is a warrior. He never runs away from problems, situations, or people. He stands strong to face them.

"Therefore, put on the complete armor of God, so that you will be able to [successfully] *resist and stand your ground in the evil day* [of danger], *and having done everything* [that the crisis demands], *to stand firm* [in your place, fully prepared, immovable, victorious]." Ephesians 6:13

Fear causes you to run away, but the Lord encourages us to stand strong, even in the face of fear and danger. Fear is a thief. It wants to steal your voice, your power, your confidence, your joy, and even your ability. Stand strong in the face of verbal and emotional abuse. It's okay to vocalize how you feel even if you are being rejected. I am not implying that you should stand there and accept abuse. However, I do believe that you can stand your ground and stand in love right where you are.

Don't run away every time you don't like what you hear. Fear can take root this way. You don't have to force anyone to listen to you, either. Your voice is being heard in the spiritual realm. Use your voice and your power to speak against the spirit of fear. God loves you, and fear is not stronger than love.

"For God did not give us a spirit of timidity or cowardice or fear, but [He has given us a spirit] *of power and of love and of sound judgment and personal discipline* [abilities that result in a calm, well-balanced mind, and self-control]." 2 Timothy 1:7

I learned this lesson the hard way. My natural reaction was to run away from my husband every time we'd fight. I was either fueled by anger or fear. I would pack my kids up and leave. I already had my mind set on divorce, so running away felt appropriate.

After all, he was the source of all my pain. I didn't realize that my pain was a battle between God and Satan. The devil was using it to destroy me, but God had a plan to save me and prepare me for my purpose. It was very disappointing to hear the voice of the Lord telling me to go home. I never liked it when he told me to stay. So many times, I doubted the voice of God. In my heart, I knew it was God, because I felt convicted if I didn't go home immediately.

Now, I can see why God was telling me to stay. Besides the obvious reason of saving my marriage, God was teaching me to stand in the face of fear. I was learning how to stand and face my problems. I had to stare my troubles in the face and trust God to deliver me. This place is a breaking point in relationships and fellowship with God. If you don't have faith or trust in his plan, you will abandon fellowship with him. This place is so fragile. Your livelihood seemingly hangs by a thread. You will see what you are truly made of, and this place will show you what level your belief system is at. Ultimately, you're being pushed past your level of ability. You are being pushed past your level of love and comprehension. This is where the extension of God's love and compassion comes in. If you let him move in your heart, his love will extend your ability to love people unconditionally and help you to operate in self-control. This behavior pleases God, and it is a representation of his character.

Another reason God was telling me to stay was because he was challenging my faith. How far are you willing to go with God? I believe ALL troubles and hellish situations are part of God's design. He allows them to continue when you want them to end. He keeps you in the fire so that you will seek him at a greater level. If the problems ended, then your prayer life would stay mediocre. How can the body of Christ rise to purpose with mediocre faith? The world doesn't need more mediocre faith.

The world and the people in it need revival! Revival happens when renewed people testify about God's goodness! God understands this well, so he sustains you while you think you are dying. He strengthens you where you think you cannot take anymore. He brings peace to your thoughts when you think you are losing your mind. Satan is a master manipulator, but God is a master motivator! If you let him, he will motivate you to rise to the next level and walk right into your destiny. I encourage you to stand with God and face your situation!

Contrarily, maybe you're not in a close relationship with God. Perhaps you are a believer, but you don't pray and fellowship with God as you should, or like you did in the past. Maybe you believe in God, but you struggle to receive Jesus. If that is you or you somewhat relate to this description, I encourage you to reset your belief system. You are probably being attacked—verbally, emotionally, or even physically—because you don't have the spiritual protection or coverage you need. I encourage you to develop a stronger relationship with Jesus. You can't win your battle by continuing in the same cycle you have been in. When we break down in life, it is a sign that the load is too heavy to carry. When a car stops running, it is because it needs maintenance. Let God heal, refresh, and renew you. If your situation is physical, I don't advise you to stay. Only you can determine the level of danger you are in. Remember that God always protects his children.

The key is to make sure you are a child of God so that he can protect you. God can change anyone, but you need to be in a safe environment if you suffer from physical abuse. Let God work on that person separately. Remember that consecration is separation for God's purposes. Go away if you need to, and let God heal you. God makes you stay so that he can prove there is nothing to fear in his presence. However, if it's not God's purpose for you to stay, or if he knows the abuser won't change, he will lead you to leave. Tune in to what God is saying to you. Only you can determine your next steps.

Therefore, Christ's sacrifice is so significant. He died to give us physical and spiritual protections that a life of sin doesn't provide. Jesus, the Son, put down his will and desires to fulfill the plans of God the Father.

In some cases, like mine, when you experience emotional abuse, God uses it to help you rise to your level of authority in Christ. It's a hard reality. But sometimes, it pleases God (or satisfies his desire) when we are in challenging positions. It doesn't please him to see us suffering.

Still, it satisfies him when he knows you will trust him and allow his plans to continue even when it hurts.

"Yet the Lord was [a]willing
To crush Him, [b]causing Him to suffer;
If [c]He would give Himself as a guilt offering [an atonement for sin],
He shall see His [spiritual] *offspring,*
He shall prolong His days,
"And the will (good pleasure) *of the Lord shall succeed and prosper in His hand."* Isaiah 53:10

The revelation of Satan's agenda is incomplete without revealing the demonic spirits behind verbal/emotional abuse. When revealing these spirits, highlighting demonic activity is not the primary purpose. The sole focus of this revelation is to help you identify spiritual warfare and teach you how to win. I recommend Apostle John Eckhardt's prophetic books and teachings as resources to learn more about these demonic spirits, their assignments, and specific prayers to defeat them. Emotional/verbal abuse is a secret weapon that Satan uses in warfare. He is willing to win no matter what the cost. He is relentless and downright cruel with this approach. His hatred for us should signify how much God loves us. It should also indicate the level of glory prepared for our individual stories.

The demonic spirits behind emotional abuse desire you to forfeit wholeness and stability in Christ. They want to steal your identity and impart a false identity, causing an identity crisis. How can you walk in your destiny if you do not know who you are? How can you fulfill your divine purpose without knowing who you are called to be on Earth? Emotional abuse gives direct access to your soul. Your soul is made up of your mind, will, and emotions. If your soul is damaged, your spirit cannot grow. Satan and his demons know this. That is why emotional abuse is a secret weapon. Sometimes it is subtle, and often normalized, but it has damaging and traumatic effects that often delay or even prevent women from fulfilling their destinies.

DEMONIC SPIRITS HIDING BEHIND EMOTIONAL ABUSE

1. **Spirit of Rejection**: Apostle Eckhardt wrote a whole book about this spirit. Rejection makes you feel misunderstood, unwanted, and alone. It can cause depression, heaviness, isolation, anxiety, anger, and more. Rejection is a demonic force that causes division and detachment in relationships. This is not the work of God, because the Bible declares unity and agreement. The demonic kingdom uses the negative words and actions of others to reject us. If the rejection is deeply rooted in your spirit, you will lose your sense of belonging or your sense of self. This notion is summed up in phrases like "black sheep," "outcast," "outsider," and "loner."

2. **Spirit of Witchcraft:** There are many layers behind this spirit. For the sake of this written work, I will only focus on the relevant characteristics of witchcraft. Astrology, emotional manipulation, and control are all forms of witchcraft. This spirit uses powers outside Christ to operate in the natural and the supernatural realms. Any power that does not acknowledge or operate under the blood of Jesus is considered witchcraft. Witchcraft events can range from physical miracles to reinforced behaviors. Therefore, emotional manipulation occurs when someone uses their words (outbursts, bullying, yelling, crying, etc.) to provoke you into a specific behavior. They manipulate your emotions because you have been programmed to carry out particular behaviors when you

hear triggering words. God does not deceive us into performing specific actions. His love, faithfulness, and goodness cause us to respond to his instructions and commands. Controlling a person's behavior works the same as emotional manipulation. They work together. When you are being manipulated, essentially, you are being controlled. Again, God does not control us with force, deceit, or manipulation. He gives us free will to choose our responses, actions, and behaviors. Even when it means disobeying him, he allows us to choose.

Astrology is related to idolatry, or the worship of false gods. Essentially, when you believe in the power of planets and stars, they take on the role of God. Astrology also provides answers to daily life and insight into the future. This is considered witchcraft. The Bible says that God is an ever-present help.

God is ready and able to answer any questions we could ever have. We must be accepting if he decides not to answer. He always knows what is best for us. It may not be best for us to receive specific information in certain seasons of our lives. Prophecy usually involves futuristic happenings. By following daily horoscopes, I accepted false prophecies and allowed the spirit of witchcraft to steal my identity. It led me into tarot cards and palm readings. This is all false prophecy because these tools use demonic powers to receive answers and insight about the future. Rejection, witchcraft, and other spirits form a diabolical alliance that opens the door from one spirit to another. Because I considered myself the "black sheep" and a "loner," it was easy to identify with subtle appearances of witchcraft in my life. Witchcraft is a sneaky spirit. Denounce these forms of it from your life today.

3. **Spirit of Fear/Intimidation**: Fear is a gripping spirit. In this regard, it has snake-like characteristics. Fear grips you in the same way that an anaconda would. This giant snake gets a tight hold and squeezes the life out of you. That is what fear does. It paralyzes you and sometimes makes you feel like you can't move. Have you ever been frozen with fear? Fear also steals your power, your confidence, and your voice. This spirit understands that there is power in your voice and in your faith in God's ability. Intimidation is best friends with the spirit of fear. Intimidation is more indirect than fear. It does not paralyze you, but it does steal your confidence. Intimidation causes you to second-guess yourself, and it shrinks your voice. It doesn't mute you entirely but restricts your willingness to use your voice. I like to think of fear and intimidation as bullies in the spirit world. Victims of bullies aren't usually quick to speak up because they are so afraid! They threaten you, take advantage of you, harass you, beat you up, and force you to be silent while it is happening. Don't let fear and intimidation steal your testimony! Remember, God has not given us a spirit of fear!

4. **Insecurity/Low Self-Esteem:** Insecurity and low self-esteem are seen in various forms worldwide. It can be seen in how women dress, how men approach women, or even how people conduct

small talk. Sometimes we bring attention to our insecurities by mentioning how fat we are, how short our hair is, or how ugly our skin is. These spirits aim to shatter self-image and reflect deep-rooted brokenness. Brokenness must already be present, which is why low self-esteem and insecurity can embed themselves deeply into your soul. If you are incredibly insecure about what you look like and who you are, then you can't walk in the fullness of God's love, nor can you be confident in God's ability. The negative words from emotional abuse cause us to focus on the bodily flesh, and God is not pleased with the works of our fleshly body, only with faith. These spirits also cause self-doubt and loss of self-respect. Just like the demonic spirits before them, they desire to steal your identity and leave you void of a true sense of self. However, this attempt at identity theft is more personal in its approach. That is why verbal/emotional abuse effectively achieves its purpose.

Nevertheless, God wants us to be confident in knowing that he created us perfectly. God created us a certain way, and when we permanently altar that creation, ultimately, we alter the plan of God. Satan knows that God's plans are eternal. When we make permanent changes to our appearance, we run the risk of permanently altering God's eternal plan. Remember that God made us in his image, and his image is perfect, with no flaws. Our attitude may be flawed, but God looks at us with perfection in his eyes.

5. **Serpentine Spirit:** The serpentine spirit has constrictor-like characteristics. It does the same things in the supernatural and

the natural. It has gripping and choking capabilities. When this spirit is present in relationships, it can feel like you can't breathe. Maybe your creativity is being smothered; maybe you never have space or alone time; perhaps you feel your partner is overbearing, constantly breathing down your neck. Your privacy and boundaries may have been hijacked. Maybe the relationship has become more co-dependent than it should be. Once the snake has a grip, it does not let go until death occurs. Perhaps you have received threats, or you just feel the sting of the grip. This spirit is vicious and very selfish. It just wants to eat, and you are the prey.

6. **Crocodile Spirit**: The crocodile spirit uses his mouth to attack. He is brutal and has a ferocious bite. This is seen through the sudden attacks of verbal abuse.

    Crocs study their prey and go unseen until they suddenly attack. This explains why verbal attacks can occur unexpectedly. They come with a low blow and bite where it hurts, just like the crocodile. Cruel verbal attacks will bring up your past or even something you are dealing with in the present. This spirit uses your secrets against you. Someone under the influence of this spirit will bring up everything you ever told them in confidence. The croc wants you to feel the pain and shows no mercy in the attack. The croc can survive in water and on land. This shows the spirit's ability to maneuver back and forth between scenarios, indicating that the croc is versatile. He can attack you in more than one place or area. This spirit will use its mouth in public, at home, on vacation, or even at work. It never stops; you are under constant verbal attack. This evil spirit never rests. Like the snake, he is always out for the kill. However, the crocodile grips you with its mouth. The croc's strength is in its words. It is relentless with what it speaks. At some point, you may have normalized the act of being under constant attack.

I became so frazzled by verbal attacks that I started hearing negativity whenever my spouse or mother spoke. It even trickled down to co-workers and associates. The croc spirit was twisting the words I heard and making them sound like attacks. I could be anywhere and become triggered. Crocodiles will twist their prey around and around until the twisting snaps the bones of the prey and they can eat it. The spirit is the same way. It will twist the very words you hear and make them sound negative; in reality, the words are spoken with a different meaning. This led to many unnecessary arguments in my house. This spirit left me unhinged, unstable, and full of misery and anger.

7. **Leviathan:** Psalms 74:14 describes Leviathan as a multiheaded sea monster killed by God and given to creatures in the wilderness as food. You may experience chaos in many different areas when this spirit is present. This is a representation of the multiple heads that it carries. Trouble can break out in your finances, relationships, home, work, vehicles, and anything else attached to you. It usually happens all at once. This spirit brings much chaos and confusion. It is a fierce attack that carries a sea of problems at once. It makes

you feel like you are drowning. Things become very chaotic and confusing.

The host of this spirit can be very calm while all hell is breaking loose, and you are left trying to fix all the problems. The host could even make things worse by bringing more chaos, confusion, or negativity to your mountain of problems.

8. **Narcissistic Spirit**: Narcissism is an excessive interest in or admiration of oneself and one's physical appearance. Synonyms for narcissism include vanity, self-admiration, and self-absorption. You can immediately see the difference between narcissism and low self-esteem. Narcissism is the process of thinking too highly of oneself, and low self-esteem is thinking less of oneself. Narcissism is so self-absorbed that it makes the people involved shrink so that the narcissist can expand. This is also considered egotism. As I mentioned, sometimes abuse is not about the victim but the abuser.

In this case, the abuser needs to feel bigger—this is the perfect opportunity for narcissism to reveal itself. In psychological terms, narcissism can be defined as selfishness, involving a sense of entitlement, a lack of empathy, and a need for admiration, characterizing a personality type. Simply put, this spirit is selfish to the core. It steals any kind of shine, esteem, confidence, talent, creativity, or praise that belongs to you. If the spotlight is yours, this spirit will snatch it to highlight the host instead. The host of this spirit is always self-seeking. The Bible makes it clear that this is not a characteristic of love. It seeks to belittle all of your work or accomplishments to highlight its own. In a relationship, it can seem like a competition of who can do things better. The host of this spirit competes with you in private. Their insecurity causes them to desire your supernatural ability or even your lifestyle. If you accomplish something, the host has to prove it can do it better or faster. This spirit will leave you questioning yourself. Am I good enough? Am I pretty enough? Can I achieve this goal or pursue that goal? Yet another spirit sent to compromise your identity.

9. **Spirit of Perversion**: This is a taunting spirit that mocks, provokes, and aggravates you. It is crooked and wears two faces. Perversion is related to injustice, meaning its motives and intentions are based on wrongdoing. This spirit is in effect when someone is intentionally offending others. It is associated with crime, misconduct, and sin.

In its corrupt nature, it perverts God's original intention for sex and it mocks sexual violations such as rape, molestation, and assault.

In marriage and relationships, it steals intimacy and replaces it with masturbation or other forms of self-pleasure. It can even cause infidelity. This spirit uses dirty language and can make you feel unclean with its spoken words. Emotional and verbal abuse is the perfect tactic for this spirit.

Chapter 3

IDENTITY THEFT

After revealing the demonic spirits behind emotional abuse, it is easy to see that there is one common factor: IDENTITY. Every evil spirit mentioned is after your personal and spiritual identity. The kingdom of darkness understands the importance of your identity. There is no wisdom or inspiration, no resource or title that is more important than your identity in Christ Jesus. Your identity in Christ is all you need to succeed in life and win spiritual battles. Everything else hinges on this discovery. Psalms 34 says the believer will lack no good thing. According to Psalms 23, we should not need anything because the Lord is our shepherd. The shepherd feeds, guides, and shields the sheep. These scriptures imply that we have all we need by simply having the spirit of Christ. That is what identity in Christ does for us. It feeds, guides, and shields us, providing all our needs.

> *"But first and most importantly seek* (aim at, strive after) *His kingdom and His righteousness* [His way of doing and being right—the attitude and character of God], *and all these things will be given to you also."* Matthew 6:33

Search after your identity in Christ first, and everything else will follow. Finding your identity in Christ means finding your place in Christ. It means finding your plan, purpose, and position in Christ. Who are you in the body of Christ? What is your level of authority? What did God create you to do? Whom are you called to help? All these questions help to define your identity. Seek God in prayer for these answers. His answers will determine your personal and spiritual identity. Consciously receiving the benefits of salvation causes you to find your divine identity in Christ. When you get saved and accept Christ into your life, you receive the benefits of salvation. That is why believers can speak the word in faith and expect results. The benefits of salvation include love, healing, forgiveness, provision, divine protection, boldness, righteousness, joy, freedom, sobriety, creativity, and the greatest gift of all—Holy Spirit.

There are many other benefits to accepting salvation. The more you walk with Christ, the more you will acknowledge the benefits of living a clean, saved lifestyle.

Another type of identity is personal identity. It includes your personality, thought patterns, and attitudes. Personal identity comes from the natural sense of self that God gives us. Naturally, we know the type of person we are. We usually know if we are introverted or extroverted. We know if we like to laugh and be silly or if we are more serious and structured. These are all personality traits, and various other personality traits can make us who we are. Life experience can influence our personality traits, but a lot of it is usually natural. Your personality can also include your talents, behaviors, and skills. Because of this, we can classify some people as having enthusiastic personalities and others not so much. This is also why we find ourselves attracted to some personalities and unable to tolerate others. It's because there are differences in everyone's personality. There are differences in the way God made all of us. These differences cause each one of us to be unique in our own ways. If Satan can steal your uniqueness, he can steal your identity. That's why one of his favorite tactics is to force everyone to blend into the crowd and follow trends. This is illustrated in the entertainment industry, where identity or *artist image* is strategically created. Identity theft is also exposed when men and women are encouraged to conform to the same stylistic standard of pop culture.

Your spiritual identity is more important than your personal identity. Our spiritual identity should be highly esteemed because the supernatural impacts the activity of the natural realm. The Bible says that the prayers of the righteous avail much. This means that God hears and answers the prayers of his children. So, when we pray in the supernatural, it can alter or change things in the Earth. Attaining your spiritual identity can defeat generational curses and provide divine protection for your family and loved ones. Christ gives us the opportunity to become real-world changers. Because we choose to take on the identity of Christ, we receive the glory of walking in his power.

Your spiritual identity can change your atmosphere. Where some environments were once intolerable, you can now speak to the environment and watch it change because of you. Some significant advantages of finding your spiritual identity are receiving the love of God and taking on his character. God is kind, faithful, and merciful. You can display these characteristics when you find your true identity in Christ. These are probably characteristics you were never able to walk in during your former life indeed.

Before we find Christ, everything is about us, and that story gets boring quickly. Everything is dark and doom and gloom. Our life-story is usually full of tragedy, trauma, and sadness. But when we accept the light of Christ, that changes in an instant. It's like a flower that blooms overnight. Everything becomes so beautiful. Everything becomes possible with Christ. That's the power of a new identity. That's the power of spiritual identity in Christ.

"Therefore, if anyone is in Christ [that is, grafted in, joined to Him by faith in Him as Savior*], he is a new creature* [reborn and renewed by the Holy Spirit]; *the old things* [the previous moral and spiritual condition] *have passed away. Behold, new things have come* [because spiritual awakening brings a new life]." 2 Corinthians 5:17

> *"Listen carefully; I am about to do a new thing,*
> *Now it will spring forth;*
> *Will you not be aware of it?*
> *I will even put a road in the wilderness,*
> *Rivers in the desert."* Isaiah 43:19

When God gives us a new identity, he does a new thing. We become new, and so should our lives. In the past, I struggled with this concept. I think many Christians struggle with this as well. Although I accepted Christ early in my life, I struggled with being the new creation that I should have been throughout the years. I continued with old habits and bad attitudes, and I did not let God's spirit transform me how he wanted to.

Identity crisis soon found me because I avoided the spiritual transformation available to me. The demonic alliance working through verbal and emotional abuse in my life planted deep roots of brokenness into my spirit and soul. At the time, I wrote and received letters from a prophetic church. It was a letter ministry. They often wrote to me about drug addiction and substance abuse, but I refused to receive the word because of my addiction and my thought patterns. I was deceiving myself into thinking that I did not need deliverance. I thought, "If marijuana is not a drug, then why do I need deliverance?" Because of the stronghold in my mind, I held on to believing that marijuana was an herbal plant, not a drug.

By smoking marijuana and agreeing with "smoker's ideology," I agreed with demonic principles. These principles made me unashamed to identify as a "smoker." My personal identity was ingrained in smoking paraphernalia. But it was all a lie. I was comfortable believing Satan's lies because smoking was pleasurable. The devil declared "Identity Theft" as my portion, and I eventually lost my complete sense of self and my confidence. I also lost a good amount of confidence in God. I was completely unhinged. I lived on an emotional rollercoaster, and every little thing brought out a sensitive response in me. Emotional abuse had achieved its goal of causing me to be unstable in my mind and emotions. I was angry, sad, distraught, misunderstood, and full of heaviness.

After giving birth to my first daughter, I accepted a new job position with Vatterott Career College. I thought this was an escape from the walls closing in on me at home, but there was a demonic plot and assignment to harass and terrorize me on the job. My husband still didn't understand the power of his words, and the verbal attacks were Satan's best strategy during my pregnancy. The pregnancy took a significant toll on me, and I was still struggling with postpartum depression. I entered the new position broken and emotionally fragile. Immediately upon taking the job, my attitude and patience were tested. My boss was overbearing, and this was a familiar quality that I'd been exposed to for a while. Suddenly my boss was displaying all the same qualities I was trying to escape from within my home. I didn't realize this was the peak of the spiritual warfare I encountered. Even my job became a point of contact for spiritual attacks. The harassing spirits eventually brought me to an undeniable realization. I was no longer the "good Christian" I thought I was. Life had beaten me up so bad, and demons had infiltrated my identity to the extent that I was no longer in the image of Christ. I became so carnal and worldly. I was easily angered, did not know how to submit to authority, was an emotional wreck, and refused to humble myself and pray. After finally blowing up at my boss, refusing to do the required assignment, and being publicly escorted from the building, I did not return. Previously, I had put in my two-week notice with the job, so the encounter forced me to leave earlier. I expected some deep sympathy from my spouse. Every day I told him about my experience with harassment. Instead of compassion, he seemingly blamed me.

"I already knew you were going to quit. You say it every day. I've already been preparing to go to work because I knew you would quit."

It's possible that he didn't mean it the way it sounded to my ears. But because my ears were auto-tuned to the devil's voice, it was another low blow to my heart. As usual, I didn't deal with the pain I was experiencing. I suppressed it and smoked it away. I smoked more and more tobacco products; I smoked more and more marijuana to numb the pain. I perfected the art of moving from trauma to trauma.

I was unaware that continuing to suppress things and move on without dealing with my pain would cause me to fall harder than I could imagine. I quickly found another job. I accepted a senior position at

National College. The environment was completely different. I had much more freedom, and I enjoyed the job.

Nonetheless, God did not want me to stay there permanently. I was always looking for a better career opportunity. I believed I could fund my entrepreneurial endeavors if I received the proper corporate position. I don't know how realistic that was, but God did not let my plans prosper. I was taking the vision God gave me for business and using it for my purposes. It took a burdensome and traumatic event to make me realize how deep I had sunk into the dark hole that was my life.

I got the call in the wee hours of the morning, around three o'clock. My sister was crying, "Punky, he's gone. He's dead! Punky, Quez is gone!" I threw the phone and screamed out in pain. My husband grabbed me and held me in the bed, trying to calm me so I didn't wake the kids. That night, my brother was murdered by his close friends. As if to add insult to injury, there was a video of him that surfaced on social media. In the video, he was lying in the street, dying. Death brought out the worst in my family. The spirit of division separated us for various reasons. We did not talk for almost a year. I finally broke down. My brother was dead, I was separated from my family, my marriage was in turmoil, I had a severe smoking addiction, my finances were dried up, and my husband had just wrecked our brand-new SUV. Around this time, God began revealing the narcissist spirit to me.

Finally, I started to cry out to God. I couldn't understand why he allowed my brother to die. I'd prayed for my brother to leave the street life for many years. God always promised he would save and protect my brother. He had many near-death experiences, and God continually spared his life. I always thought he was spared because of my prayers. I never considered that my mom and siblings were praying for him too. Do you see how pain can cause you to be so self-centered? If God had spared his life many times before, why was this time different? Why didn't he protect my brother? Did God renege on his promise?

I quit my job and fell into depression for a while. I lost weight because I was barely eating; all I could do was smoke day and night. God was dealing with me, and I realized that I needed to make some changes. I started to pray more and spend more time with God, but I still refused to deal with my addiction. My smoking addiction reached an all-time high. The Holy Spirit was relentless and would not leave me alone until I confessed. Once I stopped denying my addiction, things shifted for me.

Now that I am healed, I see things differently. If my brother had not died, I would not have realized that my life had become a mess. I didn't believe there was sin in my life because I prayed here and there. After all, I could still hear the voice of the Holy Spirit, and because I wasn't living the street life, I was a "good Christian." But really, I was not living a life satisfying God. Christ was displaced in my life, pushed out of his proper position. My heart was bitter, anger was my new attitude, and my ways were carnal, or worldly. I was not walking in the spirit of God. When I think of my brother, I think of him as my sacrifice. I see the salvation of God in his death. It is the same way Christ died for me. I take comfort in knowing God saved my brother a few months before he died. He gave his life to Christ at an altar call when the whole family was at church. God always keeps his promises.

Identity theft is the fraudulent acquisition and use of a person's private identifying information, usually for financial gain. In the spiritual and physical realm, Satan studies everything about us and our spirits. He examines our thoughts, attitudes, beliefs, pleasures, desires, and more. He gathers information and then offers the perfect enticement. Impure desires are usually the reason we accept an offer. Satan is slick; he doesn't deceive you all at once. Sometimes it is slow and gradual. We are usually unaware until something dramatic happens, forcing us to pay attention. That is how identity theft works. You don't always figure it out immediately when someone steals your information. When you see unauthorized charges, suspicious activity, and negative accounts, you start to pay attention! Some thieves only want to steal your credit card information.

Meanwhile, the obsessed thief wants to steal your persona! Satan wants to steal everything about you and everything attached to you! I had to hit rock bottom before I could acknowledge that my identity had been stolen. I lay in the darkest valley before I could accept the truth that I needed God's help to heal, achieve my destiny, and live a clean lifestyle.

"The thief comes only to steal and kill and destroy. I came that they may have and enjoy life, and have it in abundance [to the full, till it overflows]." John 10:10

Chapter 4

HEALING FROM THE PAIN, RESTORING WHAT WAS LOST

Why did God allow me to experience emotional abuse? How could this level of mental pain and anguish be effective in my life? The answers to my questions would come soon after rededicating my life to Christ. This low point in my life left me searching for a way to put the pieces back together. New Year's 2019 brought a spiritual shift into my life. I remember being so miserable on New Year's Eve. I was dead broke, my spouse and I were not speaking, and I was in undeniable pain. I knew that I could not go another year in the condition I was in. I decided I was ready for change.

I started connecting with online ministries and reattending church. My marriage was on the brink of divorce, and I felt God was not going to keep his promise and restore my marriage. I was struggling with the promises of God simultaneously, and I knew that I needed God to restore my life and not just my marriage. God displayed the power of his love to me by connecting me to different ministries at once. Suddenly, I was on a roller coaster, and this time, it was with

God. Some of these online ministries include Real Talk Kim, Sophia Ruffin, Prophet Zack Ausby, Apostle John Eckhardt, Apostle Ryan Lestrange, and my current church home, Kingdom Manna with Apostle Omar Morton. All of these prophetic ministries have a powerful online presence. If you need a Christian community and prophetic development, I recommend them. You can find them on social media platforms, including Clubhouse.

These ministries came into my life at different times and served different purposes. God connected me to ministries that could reach me while I was in the valley. They spoke to me, prayed for me, encouraged me, motivated me, and revealed to me the details of my purpose. I was quickly increasing in the things of God. Prayer was becoming my daily habit. He was so strategic with his placement. He connected me to ministries that developed the *prophet* in me. This was part of my destiny, and I did not know it. Up to this point, all of my creative gifts were classified as "talent." I had continuously operated in the spirit of prophecy and did not know that is what it was called.

When you grow with God, he reveals deeper things to you. He gives insight and details to your purpose and even your giftings. I was gaining so much new fresh revelation.

Although I was shifting spiritually, my problems did not go away overnight. My electricity was shut off due to non-payment. After I quit my job at National College, my husband did not immediately begin work. Maybe he resented me for leaving such good money behind, or perhaps he was just unsure about what to do. Communication was limited, so we did not talk about it. When my electricity was terminated, it brought a sudden boldness out of me. I demanded change. My home had been out of order for so long, but it wasn't solely because of the verbal attacks. I must blame myself for some of the disorders in my life.

I inherited my mother's work ethic and ambition. This quality and the fact that none of my accomplishments came easy developed me into a natural "go-getter." I worked two jobs in college; I worked before and after my pregnancies. This "go-getter" attitude caused me to be out of position in my marriage. I was too willing to be the provider. My independence caused me to stand in his place unknowingly. Spiritually and mentally, this discouraged my spouse from being the best man he could be to our family. There is nothing wrong with women working and providing. However, my heart posture was wrong.

I wanted to work for the wrong reasons. I even resented him for his lack of urgency regarding working and paying bills. I should have trusted God in this area and let him show me how to proceed. Through prayer and fellowship, I learned how to trust God to provide. I also learned how to get into the appropriate marital position. That's when God gave me answers for my husband's career path. With strategic wisdom, I presented the option of barber school. God heard my prayers for my husband, and he saw my fasting. He released my husband from the blockage associated with his driving license. His license had been suspended for years, and we could never save enough to pay the fees. God blessed him with the money through barber school! He accepted a brand-new position as a driver! It felt like a new beginning; I set the standard for our family to attend church consistently. Things were looking up for the first time in a long time.

This new boldness was helping me to open my mouth again. I was able to vocalize the pain I'd experienced in the marriage. Even if my husband didn't understand, he heard me. Even if he still couldn't receive me, he heard me. That was liberating all by itself. The changes that were taking place in me affected my husband. He never spoke about it because he is a man of little expression. I knew he was happy for me, but I could also see my deliverance was causing some friction. Through prayer and fasting, I was finally free from my addictions. It was a process that did not happen overnight or all at once. My sobriety was revealing my husband's vital need for deliverance. Now, I had to watch him fight like I fought with myself. It was a gruesome dog fight to watch. Quickly, I developed a hatred for the vices that I once loved. I found myself in a new battle.

Living with the things I hated was agonizing. I questioned why God kept letting me go through these things. I overcame one mountain just to make it to another one. Holy Spirit helped me maintain sobriety around all the same people I once indulged with. But there was another transition happening. All my family and friends who had judged me for drinking and smoking were now doing those things. Some of them even invited me to do it with them. I chose to walk this new life out all alone. I struggled, but I committed to my freedom.

While I was on the journey of sobriety, I read a book by Joyce Meyer. *Healing the Soul of a Woman: How to Overcome Your Emotional Wounds* shifted my thinking and introduced me to a deeper level of healing. Previously, the focus of my recovery was brokenness caused by others. Joyce revealed the power of acknowledging the self-hurt I had inflicted upon myself. Why did I accept the abuse for so long? Why did I agree with it? What is it in me that caused me to believe the lies? These questions shifted the trajectory of my healing. I decided to take responsibility for the role that I played in my season of abuse. I should have set boundaries, but I did not. Although I couldn't control the words that my loved ones used, I didn't have to agree with them. I shouldn't have allowed their negativity to define me. The truth is that most of what they said depicted how I already felt inside. This new perspective gave me my power back. Slowly, I was equipped to defeat the enemy in my life and empowered to rise to the high calling of Jesus Christ.

Finally, the path to my divine purpose was becoming apparent. Walking down this new path moved my heart to a new level of recognition. I was able to recognize the significance of the sowing and reaping principle. I had experience paying my tithes, but I did not understand the depth of the principle. It ran so much deeper than just paying a tenth to the church. This principle could change my financial situation and yet again change my thinking. One ministry taught me the value of worshiping God with my money and not just with my praise. Prophet Zack C. Ausby understood the power of this revelation, and he challenged my faith. Through the prophet, God encouraged me to sow large amounts of money that I otherwise would not have planted. It is essential to understand that it is not always about the amount. It is about the faith behind the amount. You can sow a small amount of money and have great faith connected to it.

In the same way, you can sow a large amount and not have the level of faith needed to put an expectancy on God. Faith, agreement, connection, support, worship, and expectancy are all aspects of sowing into the kingdom of God. The Lord took me deeper into the principle by moving me past simply paying tithes and offering. He taught me that I should be open to sow anytime he leads me to or when I receive an *on-time* word and expect to see the manifestation of it. As I began to fund the kingdom of God with my money, I saw my finances stabilize.

I'd been off work for a little while now and saw the difference in my cash flow. God didn't drastically increase my bank account. Instead, he sustained my money. He didn't allow me to go without the things I needed, and he often blessed me with what I wanted. He provided for me in unconventional ways. He used assistance programs, unexpected deposits, my husband, family members, and even people I did not know. God became my source, and suddenly my money stretched further than it did when I was working! He challenged my faith and gave me the opportunity to trust him on a greater level. He proved himself to be a healer and provider. I could have gone back to work, but God started to deal with me about entrepreneurship. He wanted me to stay home. I thought he wanted me home so I could immediately pursue the path to entrepreneurship. But he wanted me home so I could master the art of fellowship, worship, and divine partnership. I was in the presence of God at all hours of the day and night. This may seem dramatic and unnecessary, but I had to fill myself up with the word of God. Being in his presence creates an intimate relationship, the relationship brings change, and change brings revival. It is impossible to become a new creation in Christ without being in his presence consistently.

You cannot die to yourself and your old habits without God. You must make holy habits with God, or you will find yourself mixing the two worlds. You will live somewhere between pleasuring yourself and trying to please God.

Restoration came as a process, just like healing and deliverance. Over the years, I lost so much that I stopped keeping track. Every new loss was like another notch in the belt of disappointment. When you have genuinely experienced loss, God's promise of restoration seems like an undeserved gift. Maybe I deserved it in the areas where I could not control what happened to me. But in many places, I caused the loss, or the loss resulted from the sin in my lifestyle. Either way, restoration represents God's love, faithfulness, and compassion. He does not want to see his children broken, lacking, or disappointed.

"He refreshes and restores my soul (life);
He leads me on the paths of righteousness.
for His name's sake." Psalms 23:3

Before I could even seek God for restoration, he'd already promised me in his word and by prophecy. I received many prophecies that spoke of the bright future ahead of me—one full of joy, laughter, purpose, and prosperity. The only problem with prophecy is that you believe it will manifest overnight when you receive it. God has a distinct timeline and process that must manifest before the prophecy. Thankfully, God can restore your soul quickly. The scripture above defines the soul as life. God restored my life by giving me a new identity, a redefined purpose, sobriety, forgiveness, love, confidence, boldness, sustaining grace, and so much more. He did not restore my external conditions immediately. He restored me from the inside; he restored my soul. What's inside is so powerful that it shifts everything around you.

While God restored my life, he even made promises to fix things such as lost opportunities, friendships, relationships, my marriage, vehicles, monies, love, peace, support, sleep, self-care, and other materials.

Maybe you are like me and have experienced significant loss in your life. Perhaps you need God to restore your life and heal you from the brokenness, pain, and disappointment. There are many self-help tools in the world, but I guarantee no one can heal, restore, and transform you like Jesus.

Chapter 5

TRANSFORMING PITY INTO PURPOSE

My past is filled with so much mental and emotional pain. Satan spiritually raped me. He violated me in the most private areas of my life. He stole the love and intimacy in my marriage, he stole family relationships, he snatched my money and kept me bound by poverty, he stole cherished moments like college graduation and childbirth. However, that is not where my story ends. Jesus transformed my life from pity to purpose. God allowed me to endure emotional abuse so that I would seek him in a greater capacity. My experience taught me about spiritual warfare, and how to win. It taught me about holiness, deliverance, healing, and the power of love and forgiveness. I met Christ in a new way. He reimagined the word *savior*. He became my healer, provider, counselor, and friend. He became the center of my life, the very thing I need to start and finish each day. He is my aspiration and my dream. He is my intimate partner, the lover of my soul. His love fulfills and captivates me. Because of his ability, I am happy and whole.

Cleaning my life out and reshaping my routine was not easy, but it was necessary. I developed the holy habit of daily prayer and fellowship. Prayer is not about hiding in a closet or sitting in a pew every Sunday. Prayer is a heart posture. It is a stance in the spirit. It can be accomplished in a physical location; more importantly, it is a spiritual connection and conversation with God. Think about it this way: Do you always have long, drawn-out conversations with friends and family? Sometimes it is quick and easy. The point is that you stay connected with them and always converse, even if it is short. We must spend extended periods with God, but that is not always required. God is a spirit, but he is also a real person. He wants a relationship like we do. I talk with God all day long now. That is my greatest secret weapon. I'm not always on my knees in the prayer closet. I talk, sing, and worship while cleaning, showering, and even shopping. We're so profoundly involved now that he answers my quiet prayers through other people! If I'm shopping and I say to God, "Lord, I want these shoes, I never have enough money to get them, but I want them," suddenly, the cashier will forget to ring them up and put them in the bag. If I correct her, she'll say, "Don't worry about it!" This has happened to me before! The closeness you share with God brings favor, gifts, and surprises.

Early in life, God revealed prophetic purpose to me. As the years went on, the meaning of "prophetic" continued to unfold, but the details of my purpose always seemed to be lacking. I could never quite arrive at the place where I felt I was destined to be. The closer I got to God, the more that began to change. The Lord released certain words through his prophets, and I immediately knew the message was for me. I received the builder's anointing. I am sent to build an empire and legacy for my family. I am sent to build godly businesses and establishments. Maybe you are like me and have the grace to build. What are you meant to build? What gifts and talents did the Lord give you?

Suddenly, the abuse in my life had a new meaning. God was answering all the questions to which I'd long awaited answers. My thoughts shifted from beliefs of being cursed to the belief system that it was all God's plan! In prayer, God revealed to me that he chose pain as a development tool. He'd already shown a lot of this to me, but this time the depth of our relationship gave it new and deeper meaning. For once, I was okay with the idea of suffering for Christ. My pain had a meaning and a purpose. Finally, I was going somewhere. The destination I'd been searching for was in my master's brain, and now I had direct access to it! It makes a significant difference to suffer with a purpose versus suffering in circles with no end. Although I still struggled, I found a sense of peace in the realization that God is closer to me when I am weak.

> *"But He has said to me, "My grace is sufficient for you* [My lovingkindness and My mercy are more than enough—always available—regardless of the situation]; *for* [My] *power is being perfected* [and is completed and shows itself most effectively] *in* [your] *weakness." Therefore, I will all the more gladly boast in my weaknesses so that the power of Christ* [may completely enfold me and] *may dwell in me.* ¹⁰ *So I am well pleased with weaknesses, with insults, with distresses, with persecutions, and with difficulties, for the sake of Christ; for when I am weak* [in human strength], *then I am strong* [truly able, truly powerful, truly drawing from God's strength]." 2 Corinthians 12:9-10

> *"After you have suffered for a little while, the God of all grace* [who imparts His blessing and favor], *who called you to His eternal glory in Christ, will Himself complete, confirm, strengthen, and establish you* [making you what you ought to be]." 1 Peter 5:10

I would not have known his gracious love if it had not been for the abuse, the struggles, and the pain! How would I have learned to pray or experience the wonder of his presence? I would not have encountered the ability of his strength. And the beauty is that I was covered all along! He did not allow any physical harm to come to me. He did not allow me to experience anything that he could not restore. He knew he gave me a mighty anointing to build, heal, and set others free. This power is voice-activated, and I learned to speak fire because I was developed in the fire. By his strength and power, I can walk in perseverance and endurance. Endurance is found in your ability to withstand spiritual warfare. Perseverance is the ability to stay motivated and be diligent in the fight. God made me durable and persistent, refusing to give up, resisting the temptation to quit, and resisting the same evil spirits that resisted me.

> *"Consider it nothing but joy, my brothers and sisters, whenever you fall into various trials. Be assured that the testing of your faith* [through experience] *produces endurance* [leading to spiritual maturity and inner peace]. *And let endurance have its perfect result and do a thorough work, so that you may be perfect and completely developed* [in your faith], *lacking in nothing."* James 1:2

> *"Endurance produces character, and character produces hope. Now, this hope does not disappoint us because God's love has been poured out into our hearts by the Holy Spirit, who has been given to us."* Romans 5:4-5

I'm no longer in prayer because I'm in pain! Now I'm in prayer because I'm in love! God is the greatest love! No love can compare! He took my husband's affections away to prove that his are greater.

They are eternal, and none can compare! Nothing can fulfill you like the love of Christ, not even self-love. This is vital information for wives and women who seek more intimate love but cannot find it in themselves or their partners.

You can find the best romantic love that exists, but you will still feel as though something is missing. No worldly love can replace the spiritual love you were made to give and receive from God.

Once you experience God's sovereign love, you will inevitably encounter the power of repentance. It is a spiritual tool that is often overlooked. Repentance brings reconciliation, restoration, favor, answers, forgiveness, and closure. The Lord revealed through Joyce Meyer's book and other ministries that I needed to repent for some things. He was not telling me to repent for the usual stuff, like smoking or drinking too much. He was encouraging me to repent for self-hurt. I repented for accepting emotional abuse, and it set me free. In God's eyes, it was sinful for me to accept anything less than the goodness of his love. Of course, every love is less than his, but I understood the point. I should not have identified with the falseness or the lies of emotional abuse. I should not have hurt myself in that way. God's word says we are a royal priesthood, co-heirs with Christ, and the apple of his eye. God expects us to live at a level that represents our prestige in him. I also repented for selfish ambitions. This was so liberating because

I could finally give up my plans willingly. I surrendered my idea of who I should be and my career plans and received peace. Sometimes it's too much pressure trying to live up to your expectations of who you should be and what level your career should be on. There is even more pressure on you when you are married with kids. It's so tempting to abandon all of your responsibilities and pursue your dreams and talents. But when you receive Christ, you can rest assured that you will succeed! You don't have to worry about your career's *when*, *where*, or *how*. All you need to know is *what*. What are you supposed to do? God will help you build from there!

I used repentance as an instrument to spring clean my life. My husband's verbal attacks always provoked a volatile reaction from me. Even under attack, the Lord was teaching me his character. He soothed me and taught me the ways of his love. The Lord was growing me and stretching my attitude beyond my natural ability. Now, I was taking on his character's holiness and compassionate love. I repented for reacting in rage and anger. When I was being provoked that way, I responded naturally. I realized I did not trust God to justify me in those moments. I did not know how to trust God to fight my battles.

I could not accept the peace of God because I did not have the appropriate level of confidence that God would handle the situation or show me how to handle it.

As I matured spiritually, I apologized to my husband for my reactions. In the past, I called the police a few times, hoping they would escort him out of our house. I was so angry at his disrespect and unloving words at those times. His aggression toward me was relentless. Even when I walked away, he would follow me and continue the argument. If I asked him to leave, he would refuse. If I tried to move his stuff out, he would move mine.

Although things never got physical, sometimes I worried that they would. He would yell so loud and curse for prolonged periods with no regard for my mental state. There was no calming him or quieting him. Most of the time, I didn't know what to do except match his energy. So, I cursed and yelled too. When I felt I was backed against a wall with no other options, I would call the police because my family couldn't calm him down either. He would be so enraged, and I could never understand why it was all toward me. It was so personal. So, out of fear and desperation, I made some bad decisions. When it was all over, I would go into a dark sadness. I didn't know it was a wicked spirit attempting to contact me. It fed off my shock and dismay. I did not know that God allowed these spirits for my good. He is so powerful that even evil spirits operate under his command! Indeed, the devil was trying to kill me, but God was intriguingly involved, only allowing those demons a specific time and space to terrorize me. This part of my life is bittersweet.

Once I learned what emotional abuse was all about, I realized that my husband was suffering too. My reactions and my negative words were triggers for him too. Calling the police on him, constantly telling him that I wanted a divorce, reminding him that I was paying the bills, and not allowing him to provide the way a man should, were all triggers. I lacked respect for his organizational skills because I confused them with his controlling ways. He was not controlling in an abusive manner. He was controlling uncompromisingly. He is an avid organizer, and it constantly bothered me because I wanted to do things my way. God revealed to me that my husband was bringing order to our home, and I should respect that.

The truth is that God gave me a wonderful husband who has many great qualities. I became so engulfed with the bad that I forgot how to see the good. I had to start looking at my husband as a man with flaws, just like any other man. I learned to see him as a gift that the devil was trying to steal and an assignment from God.

When I received him as such, my prayer life advanced. Now, I stand in the gap and pray for him. I learned how to speak life over my husband and against any demonic assignment concerning him. Finally, I understood that the devil wanted to kill my husband too. In the spirit, my husband is just as valuable as me. God has placed a builder's anointing over his head too. Satan had an assignment to destroy his destiny the same way he wanted to kill mine! Divine marriage carries a heavenly agenda. Satan needed to destroy us before we reached the high place in Christ! There's no worse attack on the demonic kingdom than a married couple advancing a godly agenda! God declared war on Satan's kingdom through my marriage, and we didn't even know it! He already knew we would win! Understanding, operating, and being confident in my identity in Christ feels so good!

Chapter 6

OVERCOMING VICTIM MENTALITY, WALKING IN VICTORY

My life experiences should have left me void, empty, and cynical. Mental illness should have overtaken my mind. I should be too ashamed to tell my story because darkness and pain were my only friends. The love of God is so powerful that it can revive and re-energize you. My zeal and energy for life should be depleted, but I stand strong, full of peace. The damage the enemy tried to do to me only drove me to my destiny. I can walk and talk confidently in Christ Jesus, knowing that my story displays his glorious power.

However, when we choose not to acknowledge God in our lives, the pain and trials of life will continue to chip away at our souls and cause us irreparable damage. Without God, we risk losing our divine purpose and destiny. Without the spirit of Christ, we accept less than what is predestined for our lives. If we continue life's journey without God, we accept things like sickness and poverty. Once we settle into the idea that we can't achieve our dreams or don't deserve anything good, we lose the total value of our existence. Thank God for saving grace that transforms us from a victim mentality!

Now my life has so much meaning, and I genuinely understand that victory is available in any circumstance. The secret to walking in victory is prayer and worship. Praying in the spirit is a secret weapon. It's a sure way to walk in victory. By learning this secret, I've been able to claim victory even when the opposite is happening in my life. Having a "kingdom" mindset suggests that with the power of Christ, we don't have to wait until our circumstances change to agree with the decree that things will change. In fact, Christ tells us the opposite! Christ gives victory to the weak and those who have impossible situations!

> *"I can do all things* [which He has called me to do] *through Him who strengthens and empowers me* [to fulfill His purpose—I am self-sufficient in Christ's sufficiency; I am ready for anything and equal to anything through Him who infuses me with inner strength and confident peace.]." Philippians 4:13

> *"You will also decide and decree a thing, and it will be established for you;*
> *And the light* [of God's favor] *will shine upon your ways."* Job 22:28

God's word is a loving illustration of his desire to see us victorious and prosperous. "Praying in the spirit" can take on different definitions. But my revelation hinges upon praying in tongues. When I learned this art, my relationship with God and my prayer life elevated. Some Christians may not recognize the power of praying in tongues. And the world may take it as a joke, but when a believer taps into this area of the spirit, astonishing results follow. Praying in tongues is so important to God that he laid the foundation for us to follow.

> *"And they were all filled* [that is, diffused throughout their being] *with the Holy Spirit and began to speak in other [a]tongues* (different languages), *as the Spirit was giving them the ability to speak out* [clearly and appropriately]." Acts 2:4

When believers pray in tongues, we allow Holy Spirit to pray and speak through us. Instead of us praying natural, worldly, and circumstantial prayers, the spirit prays according to the will of God. The scripture equates praying in tongues to speaking a different language. The gift of tongues is the gift of speaking God's language. When you speak God's language, you can get answers, instructions, insights, warnings, wise counsel, and prophetic encouragement (revelation of what your future holds). There is a unique intimacy that happens when you pray in tongues. You tap into the mind of God. Simultaneously and in real time, his thoughts are in the present, the future, and the past! He will speak according to what he wants you to know.

So, in this way, God is always in control. He distributes his knowledge and power according to what you need and can handle at the time. It's a divine order and so beautiful because you can't force God to move on your behalf. In those moments, you surrender by allowing God to use your voice, mind, thoughts, and spirit to speak and release exactly what you need. Sometimes, we attempt to force God to move by crying out in anger, frustration, or sadness. We pray about the same situations and needs repeatedly, as if he didn't hear the first time.

These things don't move God. He is concerned about them, but it doesn't always cause him to respond. God responds to faith. And faith is exactly what you need to speak and receive God's language. You must trust that it is his spirit speaking a new language and not you making false words and forcing sounds to come out. If you desire to develop this language, it first starts with prayer. Pray and ask God to fill you with the Holy Spirit so you can speak his language of spiritual tongues.

Another way to develop God's language is to increase praise and worship. Remember not to force anything. But spending more time singing songs or hymns to the Lord naturally draws his presence. When you are grateful to God, worship comes naturally. Everything revolves around prayer, so even if you struggle with gratitude, pray about it. When your gratefulness overflows, you will naturally desire to worship God. Once I developed these holy habits, I saw a shift in my thinking. I was able to be victorious no matter how tumultuous my circumstances were. Truly, God was with me, teaching me how to use heavenly thoughts to my advantage. Staying in his presence taught me how to rid myself of "stinking thinking." In the word, God shows us how to attain a kingdom mindset.

> *"And do not be conformed to this world* [any longer with its superficial values and customs], *but be* [a] *transformed and progressively changed* [as you mature spiritually] *by the renewing of your mind* [focusing on godly values and ethical attitudes], *so that you may prove* [for yourselves] *what the will of God is, that which is good and acceptable and perfect* [in His plan and purpose for you]." Romans 12:2

Our thoughts are powerful, and they have the power to materialize. This is deeper than the law of attraction. It is godly. It is prophetic. Everyone may not be a prophet, but everyone can operate in the prophetic. You can use your mind's eye to think it, speak it, believe it, and manifest it through the power of Christ. Some people do this without Christ. Although it is possible outside of him, it is demonic because he is the supreme power. Every other power is false, imitation, and limited in its ability. Negative thoughts are like wounds that don't heal. They never really go away. Therefore, you must consciously disconnect yourself from negativity through prayer and the word of

God. As I began disconnecting from beliefs and thinking patterns that no longer served me, I found peace, quiet, and confidence in my soul.

Through Christ, I liberated myself from thoughts like:

> "My life sucks."
> "Life is too hard."
> "I'm too tired to pray."
> "God can't hear me."
> "Things will never change; I should just give up."
> "Things never work out for me; why do I keep trying?"

The list of these negative thoughts can go on and on. It's self-explanatory why these thoughts are so damaging. Yet, God still reveals the most important reason why in his word.

"For as he thinks in his heart, so is he [in behavior—one who manipulates].
He says to you, "Eat and drink,"
Yet his heart is not with you [but it is begrudging the cost]." Proverbs 23:7

The more you agree with these thoughts, the more you will see them appear in your life. You will continue to feel tired if you keep thinking and saying that you're tired. Things will seem to get harder and more challenging if you truly believe life is hard. Whatever you focus your mind on will be magnified. This is why Satan fills our minds with lies and perverse thoughts. Sometimes, we ourselves fill our minds with junk by consuming the wrong content and information. It can even happen by associating with the wrong people. Emotional abuse should teach us the power of words and thoughts. Thoughts matter, just like words do. We must speak life and not death, regardless of the circumstance. Your words and thoughts have the power to create real, tangible change in your life.

Clearing myself from "stinking thinking" aided me in getting in line with God's vision. I was ready to do things God's way. This time, my entrepreneurial plans succeeded because my selfish ambitions were gone. I desired to fulfill my divine purpose. Because of prophetic insight, I was making strides with my projects. God gave me the idea for my podcast and T-shirt line. I completed my poetry manuscript, which was a miracle because it was an undergraduate goal that had gone unfulfilled for so long. Graduate school was also delayed and unfulfilled for many reasons. But now, it was finally working for me.

I enrolled in graduate school and finished my first semester of grad school with a 4.0 GPA while pregnant with triplets. My projects were quickly placed on hold while I carried and birthed the triplets. It took a whole year to adjust to my new life. So many things changed, but I was still eager to finish the projects I had started. But God had another plan. Again, he invited me to a greater level in his spirit. Praise, worship, prayer, and prophecy increased due to my relentless pursuit of his spirit. Day and night, I meditated on his word. I pursued the Lord between sleeplessness and teething babies, chores, errands, homework with the big kids, assignments from my husband, bill payments, and everyday life. I sacrificed so much sleep, and *rest* became a foreign word.

My husband thought I was crazy! I would never miss a social media live or a single prayer call. And that was in between my individual pursuits of God. In the past, I would have run full steam ahead with God's vision and ideas without taking the time to pursue him for the purpose. This time, I chose to build my relationship with Christ no matter the cost. And indeed, the price was weighty. Somehow, I was gaining something greater. God is so intimate. He desires a bottomless relationship with us. That's deep! Even in the midst of so many responsibilities, he was calling me to companionship with him. I was so mesmerized by what I was learning, how I was growing, and the revelation I was gaining that I didn't realize how things had changed. My marriage was doing better. The verbal attacks had diminished. And whenever we did argue, I had more self-control. Financially, God was sustaining me in unique ways. I had so much strategic wisdom concerning business ventures and entrepreneurial projects. The Lord confirmed my calling to ministry. I even took on some leadership roles. I was starting to understand the office of a prophetess, and I began to identify and accept the title. Suddenly, I was operating in the spirit of prophecy.

Now, friends and associates looked to me for prophetic words and encouragement. I was the same one who was once broken and delirious. His ways are so wonderful. He could be selfish and draw us to this spiritual quest with no reward. If he were an evil God, we would seek him and only find a mediocre level of his spirit. Contrarily, the more we seek him, he continues to reveal a greater level of his spirit. He never runs out of glory, splendor, or revelation. It is the same way with his love. There is no cap on his love for us. It only gets greater and greater. His love results in pure victory.

Walking in victory doesn't necessarily mean walking off into the sunset. It simply means you have learned how to overcome every obstacle. In real time, you can accomplish your goals despite the roadblocks or hindrances. Christ enables us to be victorious even when it looks like the opposite is happening. You can achieve greatness in the middle of chaos. I stopped dibbling and dabbling in the world and accepted my place in the victory seat. That is how I shook the victim mentality and walked in victory.

Chapter 7

WOMAN OF GOD WALKING IN HER DIVINE DESTINY

It is not easy to walk in victory, purpose, or destiny. If it were, there would be no need for this guide. We all need revelation and strategic wisdom to gain the freedom and momentum required to achieve a divine purpose. Usually, the quest to reach divine destiny is full of pain and trials. It is not a path that will leave you unscathed. Change your perspective regarding the pain you have suffered and accept the revelation that God has allowed it to work for your good. Overcoming domestic violence or emotional abuse does not always require police, safe havens, shelters, and therapy. These are great tools to have, but it is possible to overcome with Christ alone. When you overcome with God, you conquer demonic spirits that can't be seen with the naked eye but can be felt by the sting of trauma. It sounds scary, and maybe it is, but God is a very present help. Don't underestimate the power of prayer! God revealed His power to me, and now I can share it with the world. In the middle of chaos, he revealed himself as a wonderful counselor, divine healer, provider, friend, parent, protector, lover, and confidant.

There is a divine purpose and plan for your life. By experiencing the challenges of emotional abuse, I found my true identity, my authority in Christ, and my divine purpose. At last, I overcame the snare of emotional abuse by developing an intimate relationship with Christ Jesus. I am convinced that this is the only way to be completely free. The spirit of Christ affords divine protection and finality. For many years, I tried to cry it away, work it away, ignore it and suppress it. I even abused various substances to aid in my advanced level of suppression.

Divorce and separation loomed around my mind like an orbit. Christ taught me that simply leaving an abuser will not always solve your life's emotional, mental, or financial anguish. You will eventually run into another abuser with a different face when you run away without healing your soul. Christ taught me that there is a better way. He taught me to trust that he can change people, situations, and problems. Even tragic forms of abuse cannot separate you from the love of Jesus. He can save and transform the abuser when it is in his will.

Therefore, emotional abuse is truly overcome by the power of the blood. Remember, transformation in Christ is a process, and God honors the development process. He has his unusual ways by which he provides quick fixes, and he can cause things or people to change suddenly. But usually, God allows us to experience the development process because it produces character, and character is not a quick fix. It takes years to develop righteous character. It may not be easy or fun, but the results are worth it because they are tangible and eternal. You need righteous character to navigate life in a godly way. Because of this, we can experience righteousness in heaven and on earth. Righteousness causes the enemies behind emotional abuse to be at peace with you. Overcoming emotional abuse is not an art or a science. It results from Christ-like transformation within the mind, spirit, soul, and body.

HOW TO OVERCOME EMOTIONAL ABUSE WITH PRACTICAL TACTICS

1. **Find your identity in Christ-** I have already stressed the importance of finding your identity in Christ. It is the lifeline of your ability to declare the word of God and defeat the devil. Finding your identity in Christ fills you with inspiration to change your perception. A person's identity dictates how they live, what they give, what they do, and what they accept in life. When Christ is the anchor of your identity, it is impossible to drown in life's woes or emotional abuse trauma. Let him build your character. Let him reveal your purpose. Define yourself only by his standards.

2. **Use your authority and speak the word-** God the father has every power imaginable, but many of his ways remain a mystery. In his infinite wisdom, he chose words to display the glory of his power. Using only his voice, he caused the whole world to come into existence. God was really showing the power of words by

creating Earth and everything in it. Words matter! Therefore, there is authority in your voice. God has given every person a distinct voice, and when you walk closely with God, you can use your voice to speak the word and demolish the enemy's attacks.

Holiness is what allows you to speak the word with authority! When learning to use your power in Christ, consider your level of holiness. And it's not just about physical holiness; it's also about the purity in your heart.

3. **Resist the devil, and he will flee-** The fruits of the spirit include self-control. As we grow in Christ, we gain a greater level of self-control. It takes time, but eventually, a believer should learn to sit back and trust God to solve the problem, even when it is screaming at you in the face. The devil is an attention freak. He desires to distract you daily. He believes if he bothers you long enough, you will abort your assignment and purpose in God. But the fruits of the spirit make us durable! Satan will distract you by any means necessary. Sometimes he is like the class clown. If you ignore him long enough, he will see no one is laughing, and he will shut up.

4. **Read the word out loud-** We have already established that the power of God is voice-activated. Reading the word out loud will change the atmosphere of your home or workplace. It does not have to be spoken loudly or with an overbearing tone. Even a whisper will make demons flee. The Bible refers to the word of God as being sharper than a two-edged sword. Reading the word

out loud is a one-two combo that will knock the devil and his demons out of the ring. The children of God fight with the word!

5. **Denounce the curses and pray for the abuser-** Jesus became a curse when he died on the cross for us. When he rose from the dead, he conquered every curse against us. Now, we have that same power, and we can speak against any curse and break it with the blood of Jesus Christ. When people speak word curses against you, denounce them immediately. Pray for those that curse you so that you can keep your heart clean and continue receiving God's blessings. Praying for those that curse you allows you to be released from bitterness, and it also causes the judgment of God to fall upon their head. No one can correct people like God can.

6. **Separate yourself; don't run away-** Whenever possible, separate yourself from harmful words, conversations, and hostile environments. If you pray, God will always lead you and show you when you should leave or stay. In my case, God made me stay and endure adverse environments to learn how to speak the word and watch the atmosphere change. Of course, that meant I had to let the word change me from the inside first. Separation and running away are two different things. Specific times and seasons call for you to be separated from worldly things so that you can explore the things of God in depth. You may need to separate yourself physically, but that was not my experience. I have never left my husband physically, but I was separated for God. In addition to my sobriety, I surrendered my daily activities. My husband continued

to watch coarse television shows while I stopped. I cooked for him and the family while I fasted. They would sleep while I stayed up in prayer and worship. They kept listening to rap music while I only listened to gospel. I played a deliberate part in my transformation. I consciously accepted the invitation to holiness and consecration.

Running away is the opposite of consecration. Too often, I stormed out of the house because of a heated argument with my spouse. Fueled by my intense emotions, I let the enemy drive me from the position God had placed me in. Running away usually involves division, bitterness, anger, frustration, or unforgiveness. Running away worsens the issue because the devil can corrode your heart and provoke you into sinful behavior. Separate yourself; don't run away.

7. **Acknowledge and respond to mental warfare**- Don't keep pretending that having mounds of negative thoughts is normal. Yes, everyone experiences some type of negativity or negative thoughts, but regarding emotional abuse, negative thoughts are consistent. In this battle, Satan will wage war against your mind. You may have thoughts of self-doubt, doubts about God or his existence, insecurities, self-hate, and in extreme cases, suicidal thoughts. Your mind may constantly be replaying traumatic scenarios. These are all signs of mental warfare. Don't lose hope because you can respond and overcome mental warfare with the belt of truth.

8. **Acknowledge and respond to Satan's lies**- Acknowledging Satan's lies and acknowledging mental warfare work together.

Within warfare, Satan always lies to us. Combat the enemy's lies with the belt of truth, which is the word of God. With this tactic, it is not just enough to read the word of God. You have to be specific when responding to Satan's lies. You need to identify the lies and respond immediately. Respond with scriptures that directly incriminate his lies. Here are examples:

Negative Thought, Lie: You are ugly and unattractive.

God's Word/Belt of Truth: You are fearfully and wonderfully made.

Negative Thought, Lie: You should just give up on life; no one loves you.

God's Word/Belt of Truth: You shall live and not die. I have come to give you abundant life.

At first, it is difficult to get into this habit, but remember that all things are possible with Christ Jesus. If you have trouble finding scriptures, you can google scriptures about love, truth, strength, or whatever is relevant at the time. You can use this same structure to combat mental warfare.

The enemy lies to us in various ways. He is good at lying in "vision." This means that you can hear or see something, but it is not as it seems. Because it triggers you or is emotional, you will interpret it the wrong way. This will cause an ungodly reaction like anger, sadness, or rage. "Lying in vision" is directly related to the way Satan provokes us into sinful behavior. For example, when my husband was angry with me, he would always attack my religion. Whenever I heard him on the phone talking in the same tone, I would assume he was talking about me. It caused me to have a bad attitude toward him when he wasn't talking about me at all!

Attacks of vision are rooted in witchcraft. These attacks manipulate your ears and eyes. Furthermore, they desire to manipulate your emotions and control your reactions and behaviors. In the bible, Elijah experienced a witchcraft attack. After a great victory, he was discouraged by his eyes and ears. He fled when he *heard* Jezebel was after him. He must've *seen* her coming in the spirit!

9. **Stabilize your emotions**- Combat vision attacks and manipulation by stabilizing your emotions. God desires that you are stable. Ephesians 3 paints a perfect picture of the stability we have in Christ.

> *"May He grant you out of the riches of His glory, to be strengthened and spiritually energized with power through His Spirit in your inner self,* [indwelling your innermost being and personality], 17 *so that Christ may dwell in your hearts through your faith. And may you, having been* [deeply] *rooted and* [securely] *grounded in love,* 18 *be fully capable of comprehending with all the saints* (God's people) *the width and length and height and depth of His love* [fully experiencing that amazing, endless love]; 19 *and* [that you may come] *to know* [practically, through personal experience] *the love of Christ which far surpasses* [mere] *knowledge* [without experience], *that you may be filled up* [throughout your being] *to all the fullness of God* [so that you may have the richest experience of God's presence in your lives, completely filled and flooded with God Himself]." Ephesians 3:16-19

This scripture describes the stability of God's love. Knowing a love that provides unfathomable stability, strength, energy, and fullness is wonderful. It is so clear that the love of Christ provides us with everything we need. No life experience can shake the strength of God's love. God is bold in saying that his love is the richest experience in your life! Therefore, if your emotions are stable, your mind will be stable. Most people with unstable emotions are not in a deep relationship with God. Because of this, they usually struggle and have erratic thinking patterns. These people may struggle with mental illness, anxiety, depression, bipolar disorder, or even suicide.

10. **Accept healing, extend forgiveness-** Healing, forgiveness, and trust in God also cause your emotions to be stable because they set you free from the up-and-down motion of an emotional roller coaster.

Contrarily, unforgiveness and bitterness can change your personality for the worse. They can have toxic effects on your body, mind, and soul. The pain of life can make you cold-hearted, callous, and angry, and leave you drained.

It can even make you sick in your body. The Bible refers to unforgiveness as a cancer. There is a direct relationship between bitterness, unforgiveness, and sickness. Therefore, healing requires forgiveness. Accepting healing is your way of forgiving yourself, forgiving others, and liberating yourself from the pain and bitterness. It also proves that the devil's plans against you have failed. After all you've been through, you can still have joy! The devil hates to see you with joy, but it is God's good pleasure to heal you and fill you until your cup runs over.

My experience taught me that problems, troubles, circumstances, and situations were designed to display God's natural ability. How can you showcase your talent or ability without having the opportunity to do so? How can you prove yourself if the right circumstances never present themselves? For example, a basketball player cannot prove he is the best player unless he is given a chance to play. God allows and uses the valleys in our lives to prove himself and showcase his natural ability. And his natural ability is super! He has the power to do anything, but how else will we know that God can do the impossible if he never has the opportunity to show it? You have to have impossible circumstances to get miraculous results. It took me a while to acquire this knowledge, but now that I have it, I can share this wisdom with you.

This logic shifted me to understanding and accountability. Peace came as a result of the shift, and I finally accepted that my response was my responsibility! Now, I'm intentional about protecting my peace. I always pray for the Lord to cleanse my ear and eye gates so I can interpret scenarios with his wisdom and discernment. Suppression resulted from my abuse, but I no longer suppress things.

Over time, I've learned to process what I am feeling. I say what I feel when I feel it. I use wisdom to know when I need to speak up for myself or to humble myself and be quiet. I rest in the fact that I get to choose! There is power in choice! I choose to keep my peace. I decide to increase the love walk!

I choose forgiveness and healing. While walking in divine destiny, you will encounter attacks and opposition. Now, I do a quick self-check and ask myself, "Am I bothered or unbothered?"

Because I value my peace, I usually choose unbothered! These small things keep me at peace, keep me holy, and keep me sane. I fight my battles wisely, and I'm no longer quick to take the bait of Satan. Being offended by someone's words will keep you stuck in emotional cycles.

I am free because I decided to allow Christ to navigate my life and emotions. Jesus chose my circumstances and the relationships in my life as the perfect opportunity to display his power.

My relationships and circumstances are not one-hundred percent perfect. No one's are. But the relationships in my life are finally in a healthy space because I know how to seek God, speak the word, use my authority, protect my peace, express my feelings, and communicate when necessary. Even if people choose not to change their thinking and behaviors, you can still change yours. Remember that your destiny is a journey between you and God. Not everyone will want to take the ride with you, but it is imperative for you to grow by any means necessary. My journey has brought me to Destiny Avenue. It feels good to say I am a woman of God walking in her divine destiny, and with the help of God, I broke the altar of emotional abuse in my life. I am confident you can do it too, and I encourage you to do so.

If this book inspired or gave you hope, please share your inspiration and new hope with others! Please tag me on social media when you post a positive review on your page and mine! Gift and recommend this book to someone you may know who needs this anointing to break down demonic altars in their life. Thanks for your continued support!

www.ingramcontent.com/pod-product-compliance
Lightning Source LLC
Chambersburg PA
CBHW060033180426
43196CB00045B/2652